FLEMING'S FUNDAMENTALS OF LAW

ESSAY EXAMINATION WRITING WORKBOOK
Volume 3

by

Jeff Alan Fleming
Attorney at Law

Susan Patricia Sneidmiller
Attorney at Law

LEARN TO WRITE . . . THE RIGHT WAY®

Published by: Fleming's Fundamentals of Law
26170 Enterprise Way, Suite 500, Lake Forest, CA 92630
(949) 770-7030 ♦ 1(800) LAW EXAM
FAX (949) 454-8556 ♦ WEB www.ffol.com
EMAIL info@ffol.com

Distributed by: Legal Books Distributing
4247 Whiteside Street
Los Angeles, CA 90063
1(800) 200-7112

MANAGING WRITER AND EDITOR

Susan Patricia Sneidmiller
Attorney at Law

SUPERVISING WRITER AND EDITOR

Jeff Alan Fleming
Attorney at Law

LAYOUT

Donald Bayley II
IMAGEN Company Irvine, CA.

SUMMARY OF CONTENTS

FLEMING'S FUNDAMENTALS OF LAW ESSAY EXAMINATION WRITING WORKBOOK

LEGAL MAXIM

"Out of the Facts, the Issue Arises Without Facts, There is no Issue"

I. GENERAL CONSIDERATIONS

The basic fundamentals of legal writing can be summarized in a simple statement: Legal writing is the process of applying the individual elements from the specific rules of law to specific factual situations upon which justifiable and well organized conclusions are based.

The ability to communicate clearly and concisely in the above manner must be learned and perfected. The earlier you learn the process, the more manageable your study of the law will become. The foundation upon which the technique of legal writing is built involves three distinct skills that are learned individually and then integrated with practice. The purpose of this book is to identify and demonstrate the skills that you must master as the prerequisite to producing an effective passing essay examination.

II. SKILLS TESTED

A. Analysis

Most law school examinations are presented in the form of factual situations referred to as hypotheticals. The Essay Examination Writing workbook deals solely with this form of testing.

Analysis is the ability to recognize the facts from the hypothetical that raise the legal issues and to then apply the elements from the applicable rule of law to those issues.

You must be able to read and comprehend the facts as they are given. You will soon realize that it is the facts given in the hypothetical that raise the legal issues. Because of this, you must never underestimate the importance of reading and comprehending the facts. "Fact Sensitivity" is the basis of sound legal reasoning.

The recommended steps that you should follow in sequence for proper legal analysis are:

1. Review the call of the question located at the end of the hypothetical before reading the hypothetical facts. This will help orient your thinking process to the area of law being tested. The call will often narrow the issues and parties that you are to address.

2. Read the hypothetical at least twice from a factual perspective to understand and comprehend the facts.

3. Read the hypothetical for a third time from a legal perspective at which point you may begin analyzing and issue spotting. Remember, the issue arises from the facts.

There are numerous methods that you may utilize to improve your issue spotting. You should seriously consider the following suggestions that will assist you in this area.

1. Develop approaches and issue checklists for each subject. Use the table of contents in your casebook, your class syllabus and/or the table of contents in a commercial outline as your source for development of this tool.

2. Analyze every hypothetical paying special attention to adjectives and adverbs which are descriptive words, and verbs which are action words. These types of facts are generally issues. Dates and times should never be ignored for the same reason.

3. Analyze each sentence of each paragraph in every hypothetical. Rarely, if ever, does a hypothetical contain totally irrelevant facts. With practice, you will learn to distinguish background facts from issue facts.

4. Analyze every issue by role playing each party's position. This will help you identify counter-arguments to the issues that demand extended analysis.

5. Review and write multiple examinations for each subject area in which you will be tested before sitting for your examination.

Begin the analysis of every hypothetical by allocating approximately 5-7 minutes to the steps suggested in this section.

B. Organization

It is essential for you to be able to organize your issues and arguments in a logical sequence. Students who see every issue, but are unorganized when presenting the discussion of these issues, will not pass the examination.

The call of the question will often specify the order in which the issues/parties are to be organized. If so, never deviate from the call unless absolutely necessary.

When the call of the question is very general and does not specify the order in which the issues are to be presented, (i.e., Discuss) you may organize according to:

1. The issues that each party will assert;
2. The chronology of events;
3. The sequence that is most logical based on the hypothetical. The approaches that you have developed for each subject will help you to determine the organizational sequence.

Effective outlining for 10-15 minutes will greatly assist you when organizing your issues. To conserve time, remember to abbreviate words/phrases as much as possible in your outline. You should strive to learn proper outlining as demonstrated by the model outlines that accompany each of the hypotheticals presented in this book. At first, you may become frustrated with the technique because it is new to you. Do not let your frustration get in the way of your learning process. With practice, the outlining technique will become simple and reflexive.

Do not be fooled into thinking that the time spent outlining will detract from the time necessary to complete the final written answer. When done properly, outlining will afford you the opportunity to think through and strategize your analysis and organization before you commit yourself in the blue book.

Outlining each issue as demonstrated enables you to separate major issues from minor issues, eliminate non-issues, adjust your organization when necessary, and determine how much time you must allocate to the writing of each issue. In essence, proper outlining will focus your analysis. This will ultimately save you time. For example, if you see on your outline that you have an issue that has multiple elements and facts, you will know that you will have to allocate more time to that issue than you will to another issue with fewer elements and facts.

Unless otherwise indicated, law school examinations must be completed within 60 minutes. You should strive to spend the first 10-20 minutes analyzing, organizing, and outlining before you begin writing in your blue book.

C. Writing

You must be able to demonstrate your ability to apply the elements of the applicable rule of law to facts in the hypothetical with a blend of precision and simplicity. The most efficient and effective method to accomplish this goal is through the use of the IRAC system. This method is thoroughly demonstrated in each model answer provided in this book.

To use the IRAC system, you should clearly indicate what the issue is in the form of a headnote. Follow the issue with the specific rule of law that applies. Then argue all applicable facts in relation to each and every element of the stated rule. If an element has a recognized "buzz word" associated with it, bring that "buzz word" into the discussion when addressing the facts that relate to that element.

When the analysis is completed, you must give a final conclusion. Because minimal point value is allocated to the conclusion, it should be no more than a one or two sentence summary of the stated issue.

EXAMPLE OF IRAC CONSTITUTIONAL LAW ISSUE

(I) **Equal Protection**

(R) The Equal Protection Clause prohibits (I) government regulations that (2) discriminate on the basis of an (3) arbitrary classification as (4) individuals similarly situated must be treated the same.

(A) M will ague that Suburban is a public school supported entirely by local property taxes and federal grants. The PTA is a group consisting of parents of some Suburban students. Although it is an unincorporated association, the PTA enforces school policy making it an extension of the school. Thus, the program, instituted by the PTA and sanctioned by Suburban, which limits the baseball class to boys is akin to a (1) government regulation.

The program allows boys to play baseball but prevents girls from participating even though vacancies exist. The United States Supreme Court has ruled that gender based regulations treating girls differently are (2) discriminatory. Since the program is not co-educational, it creates an (3) arbitrary classification. Further, girls at Suburban are not treated the same as boys (4) similarly situated at Suburban. Boys who want to play are permitted to enroll in baseball practice where vacancies exist but girls who want to play are not despite the same vacancies.

(C) Alice has raised a proper Equal Protection Clause challenge.

The final written product should be completed within the remaining 40-50 minutes of the examination period. If you have analyzed and organized thoroughly, you should have no problem finishing the examination within the suggested time frame.

Strive for a blue book that averages between 6-9 pages in length. Remember, it is the quality, not the quantity, of the written word that will establish success.

III. RECOMMENDED USE OF THE ESSAY EXAMINATION WRITING WORKBOOK

The Essay Examination Writing Workbook is divided into the three substantive subject areas of Constitutional Law, Criminal Procedure and Corporations. Each of these subjects is presented through five hypotheticals with corresponding model outlines and model answers. Each hypothetical emphasizes a different area of the substantive law in the designated subject. Combined, the selected hypotheticals cover the entire subject and will expose the student to the issues and arguments most likely to be tested in Constitutional Law, Criminal Procedure and Corporations during the second or third year of law school and on the State Bar Examination.

When proceeding through the materials presented in the Essay Examination Writing Workbook, you will derive the optimum benefit by following these recommended steps:

1. Read the first hypothetical presented in the section designated "Constitutional Law." For the reasons discussed previously, be sure to fully understand the call of the question and the facts.

2. When you fully understand the facts, begin issue spotting. Use the IRAC outline worksheet provided. List the issues in the (I) column, the elements of each issue in the (R) column, the corresponding facts that prove or disprove each element in the (A) column, and the conclusion in the (C) column. With practice, this technique will become automatic. Review your outline. Add any further relevant data. Delete irrelevant data. Make organizational adjustments if necessary.

3. Upon completion of your outline, turn to the model outline provided. Compare your work. Identify the issues, elements and/or key facts that you have missed. Add those to your own outline. Compare your organization. Rethink your analysis if you find errors with your organization. Adjust your outline accordingly.

   You should constantly strive to produce outlines that are similar to the model outlines in this book. Abbreviate words and phrases on your outline wherever possible to conserve time. With practice, you will develop a form of shorthand that will make your outlining time more efficient.

4. Write your final answer in a blue book using your outline as your guide. Write every issue in the IRAC format. Pay special attention to your analysis, always discussing the facts in relation to the individual elements of the rule. In this way, you will "use the facts rather than merely repeating them."

5. Compare your written answer to the model answer provided. Identify inconsistencies in your IRAC. Review your analysis carefully in comparison to the model answer looking for weaknesses in factual discussion or missed analysis. Rewrite the analysis if you have missed major facts or arguments. Then proceed to the next hypothetical and repeat the process.

The first few hypotheticals should be analyzed, organized and written at your own pace without concern for the amount of time spent on the question. It will take practice to become familiar with the IRAC form of outlining and writing. Do not rush yourself.

As you proceed to the fifth or sixth hypothetical, you will become more proficient with the suggested techniques. At that point, you should begin to adhere to the time constraints imposed under examination conditions. You will then have an appreciation for the manner in which you must pace yourself to complete the exercise within the designated time period.

Do not expect to immediately articulate every argument as clearly as that demonstrated in the model answer. The ease upon which your legal writing skills develop will depend upon how much time you devote to practicing those skills. The more hypotheticals that you write, the more proficient your writing will become.

Practice is the essential ingredient that will help you develop the skills and confidence necessary to build the foundation for sound legal writing.

IV. PREPARING FOR LAW SCHOOL EXAMINATIONS

The key to performing well on law school examinations is preparation. Preparation involves a two prong process. First, you must learn the rules of law. Second, you must demonstrate how to apply those rules in the context of a factual hypothetical. Too many students make the mistake of placing all their emphasis on the first prong at the expense of the equally important second prong. The student who allows himself to fall into this trap usually produces essays that are too law oriented, conclusary, and weak in factual analysis. The Essay Examination Writing Workbook will help you overcome these pitfalls.

Be sure to approach each hypothetical in this book as indicated. In this way, you will maximize the development of the skills that you must demonstrate for success in law school and on the Bar Examination.

GOOD LUCK!!

SECTION V

CONSTITUTIONAL LAW

CONSTITUTIONAL LAW

LEARN TO WRITE . . . THE RIGHT WAY®

CONSTITUTIONAL LAW QUESTION #1

AJAX/NED v. STATE A

The legislature of State A passed a new law requiring drivers of trucks carrying explosives on roads in State A to have "Special Driving Permits." These permits are to be issued only after very rigorous physical examinations and driving tests. The State A law also provides that only permits issued by State A are acceptable for truck drivers using roads in State A; permits issued by certain other states, all of which have less stringent requirements, are not acceptable. Under the State A law, such permits cannot be issued to persons under 30 or over 60 years of age, because statistical studies have shown that drivers in these categories have higher accident frequencies.

Assume that a federal law prohibits employers from discriminating against employees on the basis of age.

Ned, who is 62 years old, is a driver for Ajax, a truck company engaged in the interstate transportation of dynamite for construction projects in various states, including State A. Ned would normally be assigned to drive dynamite shipments from Ajax's headquarters in State B into State A, but he cannot obtain a Special Driving Permit from State A. Ned would be able to satisfy both the physical examination and driving test requirements of the State A law, but is barred solely because of his age. Ned has a driver's permit issued by State B qualifying him to drive trucks carrying explosives.

Ajax and Ned have brought suit in the United States District Court in State A against State A officials seeking to have the State A law declared invalid. The defendants have moved to have the case dismissed on the ground that the State A courts have not yet ruled upon the validity of the State A law.

1. How should the court rule on the motion for dismissal? Discuss.

2. Assume the motion to dismiss is denied. What rights arising under and protected by the U. S. Constitution should Ajax and Ned urge in support of their claims that the State A law in invalid, and what results should follow? Discuss.

IRAC OUTLINE SHEET

(I)	(R)	(A)	(C)

Model Outlines Serve As A Demonstration Only. Students Should Abbreviate Words & Phrases Whenever Possible To Keep Outline Time Between 15 - 20 Minutes.

EXAMPLE OF PROPER IRAC OUTLINE

1. HOW SHOULD THE COURT RULE ON THE MOTION FOR DISMISSAL?

(I)	(R)	(A)	(C)
ABSTENTION DOCTRINE	Federal Court Must Abstain	N a 62 year old truck driver from State B cannot obtain a Special Driving Permit under State A law to drive in State A The legislature of State A passed a new law requiring drivers of trucks carrying explosives on roads in State A to have "Special Driving Permits" These permits are to be issued only after very rigorous tests State A law provides that only permits issued by State A are acceptable for truck drivers using State A roads Permits issued by certain other states, which have less stringent requirements, are not acceptable Under the State A law, such permits cannot be issued to persons under 30 or over 60 years of age because statistical studies have shown that drivers in these categories have higher accident frequencies	No Abstention
	Case-State Statute Until Decided By State Court	A/N have brought suit in U.S. District Court in State A against officials seeking to have the State A law declared invalid Defendant's have moved to have case dismissed on the ground that the State A courts have not yet ruled upon the validity of the State A law	
	Unless Statute Unconstitutional	Law prohibits persons under 30 or over 60 from obtaining a Special Driving Permit N who is 62, is a driver for A, a truck company engaged in the interstate transport of dynamite for construction projects in various states including State A (Equal Protection violation?) N would normally be assigned to drive dynamite shipments from A's headquarters, in State B into State A, but he cannot obtain a Special Driving Permit from State A (undue burden on interstate commerce?)	
RIPENESS	Actual Injury/Immediate Threat Actual Injury	N is a 62 yr old truck driver for A, supra N would normally be assigned to drive into State A, supra N cannot obtain a Special Driving Permit, supra (threat of prosecution?)	Ripe

2. AJAX (A)/NED (N) v. STATE A OFFICIALS

(I)	(R)	(A)	(C)
VALIDITY OF FEDERAL LAW COMMERCE CLAUSE	Congress Power To Regulate Commerce	A federal law prohibits employers from discriminating against employees on the basis of age	Commerce Clause Applies
PREEMPTION - SUPREMACY CLAUSE	Constitution/Laws Supreme Law Of Land	A federal law prohibits employers from discriminating against employees on the basis of age State A law prohibits issuance of Special Driving Permits to truck drivers under age 30 or over age 60 Ned is 62 A engages in interstate transportation business in State A, supra (conflict?)	Supremacy Clause May Apply
INTENT TO OCCUPY	Congressional Intent Implied	A federal law prohibits employers from discriminating based on age State A law prohibits permits to persons under 30 or over 60 Employment discrimination v. driving regulation	No Intent To Occupy

(I)	(R)	(A)	(C)
TENTH AMENDMENT	Police Powers	State A law requires drivers of trucks carrying explosives on roads in State A to have "Special Driving Permits," supra (safety, welfare, local concern)	Valid
COMMERCE CLAUSE	States Concurrent Power Where No Federal Legislation	State A law, supra.	Invalid
	Balance State Interest	Drivers of explosives have higher accident frequencies based on age (safety, welfare, local concern?) Law not discriminatory as permits issued after rigorous PX exams and driving tests Applies to all truck drivers	
	Unduly Burden Interstate Commerce	N would be able to satisfy both PX exam and driving test requirements of the State A law Stops free flow of commerce from state to state	
EQUAL PROTECTION	Government Regulation	The legislature of State A passed a new law requiring drivers carrying explosives to have "Special Driving Permits," supra	Possible Violation
	Discriminate	Permits cannot be issued to persons under 30 or over 60	
	Arbitrary Classification	N barred solely because of his age	
	Individuals Similarly Situated	Drivers between ages of 30-60	
STATE ACTION	Nexus Test	The legislature of State A passed a new law, supra	State Action
CLASSIFY DISCRIMINATION	Age Non/Suspect	N is barred solely because of his age	No Violation
	Rational Basis	Statistical studies have shown that drivers in these categories, supra, have higher accident frequencies (safety/welfare)	

EXAMPLE OF IRAC CONSTITUTIONAL LAW ISSUE

(I) **Procedure - Ripeness**

(R) The Court will not decide constitutional questions unless the complainants demonstrate an (1) actual injury or an (2) immediate threat of an actual injury.

(A) Ned is a 62 year old truck driver for Ajax, a truck company engaged in the interstate transportation of dynamite in State A. He would normally be assigned to drive dynamite shipments from Ajax's State B headquarters into State A. However, he cannot obtain a "Special Driving Permit" from State A solely because he is 62 years old. If he drives into State A without the permit, he can be prosecuted for violating the law.

The court will not require Ned to actually violate the law and suffer (1) actual injury before it will hear the controversy. The mere threat of civil or criminal consequences to both Ajax and Ned has the tacit effect of barring Ned from driving in State A. Because of this (2) immediate threat, Ned cannot carry out the function for which Ajax hired him. Ned can demonstrate that the State A law has posed, and continues to pose, a real and immediate danger of actual injury to his present and future employment interests.

Ned's suit is ripe and the court may hear the controversy.

(C) The court should deny State A's motion for dismissal.

SUGGESTED MODEL ANSWER

1. HOW SHOULD THE COURT RULE ON THE MOTION FOR DISMISSAL?

Procedure - Abstention Doctrine

Federal courts must temporarily abstain from hearing a case involving a state statute until such time as the case is decided by a state court unless the statute would be unconstitutional.

Ned, a 62 year old truck driver from State B cannot obtain a "Special Driving Permit" under State A law to drive in State A. The legislature of State A passed a new law requiring drivers of trucks carrying explosives on roads in State A to have "Special Driving Permits." The law dictates that these permits are to be issued only after very rigorous tests, that only permits issued by State A are acceptable for truck drivers using State A roads, and that permits issued by certain other states having less stringent requirements are not acceptable. Such permits cannot be issued to persons under 30 or over 60 years of age because statistical studies have shown that drivers in these categories have higher accident frequencies.

Ajax/Ned have brought suit in the State A U.S. District Court against State A officials seeking to have the law declared invalid. State A's counsel will argue that State A courts have not yet ruled upon the validity of the State A law. Ned's challenge must first be heard in a State A court before the federal courts may review it. State A is entitled to control over its own laws. Preserving its sovereignty includes having its own judiciary interpret and rule on State A laws before the federal courts intervene. Thus, the federal court must temporarily abstain from hearing Ned's suit until such time as the case is decided by a State A court.

Ajax/Ned will contend that their suit involves two federal constitutional questions. The first question addresses the section of the law that prohibits persons under 30 or over 60 from obtaining a Special Driving Permit. Ned, who is 62, is a driver for Ajax, a truck company engaged in the interstate transportation of dynamite for construction projects in various states including State A. Ned has been denied a permit solely because of his age. This raises an issue of an equal protection challenge on the basis of age discrimination.

The second question addresses the requirement that truck drivers in State A who are engaged in interstate transportation of dynamite for construction projects have a "Special Driving Permit." Ned would normally be assigned to drive dynamite shipments from Ajax's headquarters in State B into State A. However, State A will not give him a "Special Driving Permit." Therefore, State A is effectively restricting truck drivers who can use State A roads.

This regulation unduly burdens interstate commerce. Clear federal questions arising under the Constitution are the basis of Ajax's/ Ned's suit. Since the State A statute could be unconstitutional, the federal court need not require State A to first rule on the case. Instead, Ned may immediately file in the U.S. District Court.

The federal court does not have to abstain from hearing Ned's suit.

Procedure - Ripeness

The court will not decide constitutional questions unless the complainants demonstrate an actual injury or an immediate threat of an actual injury.

Ned is a 62 year old truck driver for Ajax, a truck company engaged in the interstate transportation of dynamite in State A. He would normally be assigned to drive dynamite shipments from Ajax's State B headquarters into State A. However, he cannot obtain a "Special Driving Permit" from State

A solely because he is 62 years old. If he drives into State A without the permit, he can be prosecuted for violating the law.

The court will not require Ned to actually violate the law and suffer actual injury before it will hear the controversy. The mere threat of civil or criminal consequences to both Ajax and Ned has the tacit effect of barring Ned from driving in State A. Because of this immediate threat, Ned cannot carry out the function for which Ajax hired him. Ned can demonstrate that the State A law has posed, and continues to pose, a real and immediate danger of actual injury to his present and future employment interests.

Ned's suit is ripe and the court may hear the controversy.

The court should deny State A's motion for dismissal.

2. AJAX/NED v. STATE A OFFICIALS

Validity of Federal Law - Power Source - Commerce Clause

Article I section 8 of the Constitution grants Congress the power to regulate commerce among the several states.

The facts indicate that a federal law prohibits employers from discriminating against employees on the basis of age. Generally, a congressional act is authorized by the Commerce Clause if there is any rational basis for the regulation. Here, employment discrimination could adversely effect the channels of interstate commerce or activities that have a national economic effect. Because commerce, in the form of an interstate carrier using interstate roads, is impacted by employment discrimination, the Commerce Clause grants Congress the power to regulate this type of commerce.

Preemption: Conflict - Supremacy Clause

Article VI, Section 2 of the Supremacy Clause provides: "The Constitution and the Laws of the United States, which shall be made in pursuance thereof, shall be the supreme law of the land."

Ajax and Ned will assert that federal law prohibits employers from discriminating against employees on the basis of age. Here, the State A law prohibits the issuance of "Special Driving Permits" to truck drivers under age 30 or over age 60. This puts Ajax in the position of having to restrict its hiring of employees such as Ned, who is 62, to those between the ages of 30-60 if it wishes to carry on its interstate transportation business in State A. The State A law, in effect, conflicts and otherwise stands as an obstacle to the accomplishment and execution of the purpose of the federal law which prohibits discrimination against employees on the basis of age. As a result, it is invalid under the Supremacy Clause.

State A will rebut that the State A law prohibits the issuance of driving permits to persons under 30 or over 60. This is a state licensing regulation restricting driving privileges in State A rather than employment discrimination. As such, the State A law does not conflict with the federal law.

Therefore, the Supremacy Clause may not preempt the State A law.

Intent To Occupy

Where no express conflict exists between a federal and a state law, congressional intent must be implied from the subject matter of the federal legislation.

The federal law prohibits employers from discriminating against employees on the basis of age.

This precise language indicates that the federal government intends to occupy all aspects of employer related age discrimination where it impacts on interstate commerce.

State A will argue that statistical studies have shown that drivers under 30 and over 60 have higher accident frequencies. This is the reason it passed the law restricting these categories of drivers from carrying explosives. Thus, congressional intent to prevent employment discrimination does not apply to this situation.

It is unclear from the facts whether the statistical studies were conducted by State A officials examining accidents in State A or whether the conclusions in the studies applied to all states in general. If the studies involve accidents in State A where road conditions might differ from road conditions in other states, there would be no need for national uniformity. In this instance, the State A law merely supplements the federal law with stricter laws regarding the use of its roads by those persons driving with explosives.

The State A law will not be invalidated by the preemption doctrine.

Is the State Law Valid Under The Tenth Amendment?

The Tenth Amendment gives to the states the power to regulate the health, safety, welfare, local concern, and morals of its citizens through its police powers, where the federal government has not specifically reserved these powers for itself.

The State A law regulates the issuance of driving permits to truck drivers who transport explosives on State A roads. Because the transportation of explosives directly affects the safety, welfare, and local concern of State A citizens who could be hurt by unqualified drivers transporting explosives, State A has properly exercised its police powers by passing the law.

The State A law is valid under the Tenth Amendment.

Commerce Clause

The congressional power over interstate commerce is not exclusive, giving the states concurrent power to regulate where there is no relevant federal legislation. The court will balance the state's interest against its burden on interstate commerce.

As previously stated, State A's law regulates the issuance of driving permits to truck drivers who carry explosives. Since there is no federal law regulating this aspect of commerce, State A has the concurrent power to do so.

State A will assert that it has a legitimate interest in protecting its citizens from high accident frequencies caused by truck drivers transporting explosives. Since age has been found to be a factor in the frequency of these accidents, the safety and welfare of State A's citizens is of great local concern. Thus, State A may legislate in this area.

Moreover, the driving restriction is not discriminatory. It applies to all truck drivers, irrespective of whether they are in-state or out-of-state drivers. All truck drivers must pass State A qualification requirements based on age, physical examinations and driving tests to ensure that uniform standards are maintained. Therefore, the law does not discriminate against out-of-state truck drivers and should be upheld.

However, the court must balance the state's interest against the burden it creates on interstate commerce. Not all truck drivers under the age of 30 or over the age of 60 are high accident risks. State A's own rigorous physical examination and driving test requirements should provide a sufficient screening process to determine which truck drivers should receive a permit and which ones should not. In fact, Ned would be able to satisfy these requirements despite his being 62 years of age.

State A's demand that employers transporting explosives in State A use only drivers meeting strict age restrictions that these same employers are not subject to in any other state unduly burdens national employment and transportation. Any driver from another state who is transporting explosives through or into State A and is over the designated age, as is the case with Ned, cannot receive a permit. This unduly burdens the free flow of commerce from state to state.

The burden that the State A law imposes on employment and the free flow of interstate commerce outweighs the benefits State A seeks to achieve through the law.

Even if the court would balance in favor of State A, which is unlikely, there is no doubt that State A could accomplish its objectives in a less restrictive means by simply requiring drivers to pass its physical examination and driving requirements as is the case in other states. This should be an effective indicia of driving qualification based on skill rather than on age.

Therefore, since the State A law does unduly burden interstate commerce and less restrictive alternative means exist, the State A law should be found invalid and unconstitutional.

Equal Protection

The Equal Protection Clause prohibits government regulations that discriminate on the basis of an arbitrary classification as individuals similarly situated must be treated the same.

By the terms of the State A law, the issuance of a permit to drivers of explosives under the age of 30 or over the age of 60 is prohibited, irrespective of the fact that these same drivers could pass the State A physical examination and driving test requirements. Ned could pass the State A testing requirements. Yet, due to his age, he is being denied a driving permit. The State A law, through the legislative process, is a government regulation that discriminates against Ned based on age, an arbitrary classification. Ned is being treated differently than other truck drivers between the age of 30 and the age of 60 similarly situated, as they are not subject to the State A law.

Ned has raised a proper Equal Protection Clause challenge.

State Action

In order to establish a violation of Equal Protection Clause, a nexus must be shown between the alleged discriminatory activity and the state's involvement.

The legislature of State A passed the new law requiring the "Special Driving Permits." Since the law is being regulated and enforced by State A itself, a nexus can be shown to exist between the discriminatory issuance of permits and State A's involvement in enforcing of this law.

State action is present.

Classification Of The Discrimination

Age discrimination is judged by the rational basis test.

Statistical studies have shown that drivers in the age categories that State A restricts have higher accident frequencies than those drivers who are between the ages of 30 and 60. The law restricts only those drivers in specified age categories who carry explosives. Because the State is attempting to reduce the number of accidents that have a high potential for injury and death, thereby protecting the safety and welfare of its citizens, it has a rational basis for implementing the law.

Ned will counter that age, like gender, is a classification that has unalterable characteristics. People over the age of 60 have a history of being treated unequally when it involves employment and driving privileges. Therefore, the standard used to determine this type of discrimination should be intermediate scrutiny rather than the rational basis test.

Nevertheless, the court has specifically held that the aged do not satisfy the criteria related to a history of discrimination and, therefore, the state need only show a rational basis.

State A's law does not violate equal protection.

CONSTITUTIONAL LAW QUESTION #2

JONES v. EXECUTIVE ORDER

The President of the United States issued an executive order authorizing the F.B.I., without first obtaining a search warrant, to tap telephones of aliens in cases of suspected espionage or subversion by foreign powers.

Congress subsequently passed a bill prohibiting all wiretaps without a warrant, but the President vetoed the bill and Congress was unable to override the veto. Congress then passed a concurrent resolution (which does not require presidential approval) stating the sense of the Congress that no warrantless wiretaps should be permitted within the United States. Congress, over the President's veto, passed a statute permitting any federal taxpayer to bring suit in a federal district court to contest the validity of the President's executive order. No other statute affects the subject.

An action was later filed in federal district court by Jones, a citizen and taxpayer. Jones contested the validity of the Executive Order on constitutional grounds and sought to show at the trial that the F.B.I. had in fact tapped telephones in the United States without warrant and that some telephones of citizens had been tapped. Jones caused an F.B.I. agent to be subpoenaed to testify and produce records regarding the telephone taps in issue, but the President claimed executive privilege and the agent neither appeared nor produced any records.

The federal district and appellate courts ruled against Jones and the Supreme Court has granted review.

What result on all constitutional issues? Discuss.

IRAC OUTLINE SHEET

(I)	(R)	(A)	(C)

EXAMPLE OF PROPER IRAC OUTLINE

JONES (J) v. EXECUTIVE ORDER

(I)	(R)	(A)	(C)
PERSONAL STANDING	Direct/Immediate Personal Injury To Challenged Action	The President of the U.S. issued an executive order authorizing the F.B.I. without first obtaining a search warrant, to tap telephones of aliens in cases of suspected espionage or subversion by foreign powers (1st/4th Amendment violation?)	Arguable
	Remedy Will Redress	An action was later filed by J a citizen & taxpayer J contested the validity of the executive order on constitutional grounds & sought to show at trial that the FBI had tapped U.S. telephones of citizens w/o a search warrant	
FEDERAL TAXPAYER STANDING	Federal Taxpayer	J a U.S. citizen/taxpayer supra	No Standing
	Federal Taxing/Spending Power	FBI taps phones (funds from federal taxes?)	
	Exceeds Constitutional Limitation	F.B.I. tap phones (possible speech, privacy violation)	
CONGRESSIONAL STANDING	Article III-Congress Federal Statute Create Standing	Congress, over the President's veto, passed statute permitting "any" federal taxpayer to bring suit in a federal district court to contest the validity of the President's executive order An action was later filed by J	No Standing
	Legislation Constitutional	Any federal taxpayer may bring suit	
VIOLATION OF EXECUTIVE ORDER SEPARATION OF POWERS	Executive - Article II	Executive order supra	No Violation
	Legislative - Article I	Congress subsequently passed a bill prohibiting all wiretaps w/o a search warrant	
	Prevent Abuses Of Power	The President vetoed the bill & Congress was unable to override the veto Congress then passed a concurrent resolution (which does not require presidential approval) stating the sense of the Congress that no warrantless wiretaps should be permitted within the U.S.	
FOURTH AMENDMENT	Protects Against Unreasonable Searches/Seizures	Executive order authorizing warrantless wiretaps supra	Violation
	Governmental Intrusion	Executive order/FBI agents	
	Expectation Of Privacy	Telephone	
EXCEPTION TO WARRANTLESS SEARCH:			
EXIGENT CIRCUMSTANCES	Hot Pursuit Of Suspect	?	Invalid
	Loss/Destruction Of Evidence	Executive order authorizing warrantless wiretaps of telephones in cases of aliens suspected espionage/ subversion by foreign powers supra	

(I)	(R)	(A)	(C)
EQUAL PROTECTION	Government Regulation	President issued an executive order authorizing FBI w/o warrant to tap telephones supra	Proper Challenge
	Discriminate	Tap phones of aliens without search warrant	
	Arbitrary Classification	Aliens' phones wiretapped	
	Individuals Similarly Situated	Treated differently than U.S. citizens	
STATE ACTION	Nexus Test	Executive order/FBI to tap telephones w/o a search warrant supra	State Action
CLASSIFY DISCRIMINATION	Alienage - Suspect	Executive order authorizing wiretaps without search warrant of aliens supra	Violation
	Strict Scrutiny	Purposefully discriminates against aliens	
	Compelling State Interest	Suspected espionage or subversion by foreign powers	
	Least Burdensome Alternative	FBI should substantiate its evidence	
FIRST AMENDMENT FREE SPEECH	Preferred Right	Warrantless telephone taps of aliens suspected supra J contested validity of executive order on constitutional grounds & sought to show that FBI had tapped phones in U.S. without search warrant & some telephones of citizens had been tapped supra	Violation
	Not Absolute	(balance national security v. free speech)	
OVERBREADTH	Regulation Of Protected/ Unprotected Expression	Executive order supra Telephone taps of aliens supra FBI had tapped phones in U.S. without search warrant & some telephones of citizens had been tapped	Overbroad
EXECUTIVE PRIVILEGE	Implied Immunity	J caused an FBI agent to be subpoenaed to testify & produce records of telephone taps in issue President claimed executive privilege Agent neither appeared nor produced any records	No Privilege
	Compelling National Interest	Alien suspected of espionage or subversion by foreign powers	

EXAMPLE OF IRAC CONSTITUTIONAL LAW ISSUE

(I) **Procedure - Personal Standing**

(R) Article III requires that a person asserting the violation of a constitutional right must show a (1) direct and immediate personal injury due to the (2) challenged action and that (3) the remedy sought will redress the alleged injury.

(A) The President of the United States issued an executive order authorizing the F.B.I., without first obtaining a search warrant, to tap telephones of aliens in cases of suspected espionage or subversion by foreign powers. Jones will allege that the order directly violates his First Amendment right to speech and his Fourth Amendment right of privacy.

Jones can substantiate his claim by alleging that, although the order specified that it applied specifically to aliens, he had evidence which he sought to show at trial proving that the F.B.I. had tapped the telephones of United States citizens without a search warrant in its quest to reach aliens suspected of espionage or subversive activity. This creates a strong possibility that if and when Jones communicates with aliens living in this country whose telephones were tapped, his conversations would also be monitored. Such circumstances give rise to a (1) direct and immediate personal injury that could be traced to the executive order, the basis of the (2) challenged action.

Further, Jones' action of filing suit contesting the validity of the executive order on constitutional grounds is (3) the proper remedy. It will redress the potential loss of First and Fourth Amendment rights.

However, Jones cannot prove that he has personally experienced any injury to his constitutional rights. The allegation of a mere possibility of injury is not sufficient for personal standing.

(C) Therefore, the courts ruling against Jones may have been proper.

SUGGESTED MODEL ANSWER

JONES v. EXECUTIVE ORDER

Procedure - Personal Standing

Article III requires that a person asserting the violation of a constitutional right must show a direct and immediate personal injury due to the challenged action and that the remedy sought will redress the alleged injury.

The President of the United States issued an executive order authorizing the F.B.I., without first obtaining a search warrant, to tap telephones of aliens in cases of suspected espionage or subversion by foreign powers. Jones will allege that the order directly violates his First Amendment right to speech and his Fourth Amendment right of privacy.

Jones can substantiate his claim alleging that, although the order specifies that it applies specifically to aliens, he has evidence which he sought to show at trial proving that the F.B.I. has tapped the telephones of United States citizens without a search warrant in its quest to reach aliens suspected of espionage or subversive activity. This creates a strong possibility that if and when Jones communicates with aliens living in this country whose telephones were tapped, his conversations will also be monitored. Such circumstances give rise to a direct and immediate personal injury that can be traced to the executive order, the basis of the challenged action.

Further, Jones' action of filing suit contesting the validity of the executive order on constitutional grounds is the proper remedy. It will redress the potential loss of First and Fourth Amendment rights.

However, Jones cannot prove that he has personally experienced any injury to his constitutional rights. The allegation of a mere possibility of injury is not sufficient for personal standing.

Therefore, the courts ruling against Jones may have been proper.

Procedure - Federal Taxpayer Standing

A federal taxpayer may have standing to bring suit if the challenged federal action arises from the taxing and spending power and it exceeds a specific constitutional limitation on the taxing and spending power.

Jones will contend that he is a United States citizen. This status infers that he is a federal taxpayer. The funds used to support the F.B.I. in its effort to execute the telephone wiretaps without a search warrant must have been derived from federal taxes paid by citizens of the United States including Jones. Since these wiretaps are being conducted as part of a Presidential executive order, they arise from the federal taxing and spending power.

Although the expenditures may result in an infringement on Jones' First Amendment right of speech and Fourth Amendment right of privacy, his challenge only shows that the program's use of the funds is generally beyond the powers delegated to the executive branch. The expenditures do not exceed a specific constitutional limitation on the taxing and spending power.

Therefore, Jones has no federal taxpayer standing.

Procedure - Congressional Standing

Article III permits Congress to create standing by federal statute provided the legislation comports with constitutional standards.

Congress, over the President's veto, passed a federal statute permitting any federal taxpayer to bring suit in federal district court to contest the validity of the President's executive order. Jones filed an action pursuant to the statute specifically creating standing.

The federal statute allows "any taxpayer" to bring suit in federal court to contest the order irrespective of whether that person has an adverse legal interest in the controversy. Because Congress may not go beyond Article III's requirement of "injury in fact," the legislation exceeds the limits of congressional jurisdiction. The statute, itself, is unconstitutional.

Jones may not invoke standing under the congressional statute.

VALIDITY OF EXECUTIVE ORDER

Separation Of Powers

The Constitution enumerates specified powers upon the executive branch under Article II and the legislative branch under Article I to prevent abuses of power.

The President issued an executive order authorizing the F.B.I., without a search warrant, to wiretap telephones of aliens in cases of suspected espionage or subversion by foreign power. Since the United States Supreme Court has broadly interpreted the grant of power to the executive branch under Article II, it appears the exercise of the executive power is proper.

Jones will counter that the executive order impermissibly infringes upon the powers granted by the Constitution to the legislative branch under Article I. His argument is substantiated by the fact that Congress subsequently passed a bill prohibiting all wiretaps without a search warrant but the President vetoed the bill and Congress was unable to override the veto.

However, the Constitution authorizes veto power for the executive branch. The President's use of the veto is not an abuse of power. When Congress passed its concurrent resolution (which doesn't require presidential approval) stating the sense of the Congress that no warrantless wiretaps should be permitted in the United States, its action merely reflected its intent but did not effect the President's veto power over the original bill.

The separation of powers doctrine has not been violated.

Fourth Amendment - Warrantless Search

The Fourth Amendment protects against unreasonable searches and seizures by a governmental intrusion upon a reasonable expectation of privacy.

The executive order authorizing warrantless wiretaps of aliens suspected of espionage or subversion constitutes an unreasonable search. It was issued by the President and carried out by the F.B.I. Since both the President and the F.B.I. are acting in their capacities as government entities when authorizing and enforcing the order, their conduct is sufficient to show a governmental intrusion. The use of a telephone carries with it a reasonable expectation of privacy.

Warrantless wiretaps are presumed invalid unless the government can show an applicable exception.

Exigent Circumstances

A warrantless search may be conducted when officers are in hot pursuit of a suspect or when the delay caused by obtaining a warrant would permit evidence to be lost or destroyed.

The government will allege that the executive order authorizing warrantless wiretaps of telephone conversations by aliens suspected of espionage or subversion must be recorded at the moment in which they are engaged to prevent the loss or destruction of such evidence. Since the taps are being conducted in cases of suspected espionage or subversion by foreign powers, this is the only means to obtain and preserve the evidence. These conversations would otherwise be lost if the F.B.I. were forced to guess when a telephone call would be made in order to secure a search warrant prior to that telephone conversation.

Yet, national security based on suspected acts of espionage or subversion has never been considered an emergency sufficient to outweigh the strict search warrant requirement in cases where telephones are to be tapped. United States citizens and aliens are entitled to a reasonable expectation of privacy in their use of the telephone. This right is not outweighed by unsubstantiated F.B.I. suspicions.

Exigent circumstances will not apply. The executive order violates the Fourth Amendment's prohibition against unreasonable searches and seizures.

Equal Protection

The Equal Protection Clause prohibits government regulations that discriminate on the basis of an arbitrary classification as individuals similarly situated must be treated the same.

The President issued an executive order authorizing the F.B.I. to tap telephones of aliens without a search warrant. The order was issued by the President and carried out by the F.B.I.. Since both entities are acting as extensions of the government and are enforcing a government policy, a government regulation exists.

The order created different wiretapping standards between aliens and United States citizens. Such differences in standards are discriminatory. They also result in an arbitrary classification. Aliens are not treated the same as citizens similarly situated whose phones require a search warrant when tapped.

Therefore, Jones has raised a proper Equal Protection challenge.

State Action

In order to establish a violation of Equal Protection Clause, a nexus must be shown between the alleged discriminatory activity and the state's involvement.

The F.B.I. enforces the executive order. This created a significant relationship between the federal agency responsible for its implementation and the cooperation from the state in which it is carried out. Such direct significant involvement between a government agency and the state where enforcement is conducted is sufficient to prove a nexus between the discriminatory order and the state.

State action is present.

Classification Of The Discrimination

Alienage is considered a suspect classification for which government action is subject to strict scrutiny and the government must show a compelling state interest and the least burdensome alternative available.

The executive order authorizing telephone wiretaps without a search warrant are being conducted against aliens, a suspect class. The government's objective is to protect national security by preventing suspected espionage by aliens.

The wiretaps are authorized, not only in bona fide cases of alien espionage or subversion, but also in cases where such activity is merely suspected. A mere suspicion without more proof of actual espionage or subversive activity does not automatically support a breach of national security. Thus, the government order purposefully discriminates against aliens and is subject to strict scrutiny. It does not appear that the government has a compelling state interest to protect mere suspected subversive activity.

The government would rebut that, because of the broad and exclusive federal power over foreign affairs and immigration, federal government action affecting aliens is subject only to the rational basis standard. The warrantless wiretaps on telephones of aliens suspected of subversion is rationally related to the protection of national security.

However, as discussed supra, the states in which the warrantless searches are carried out will be directly involved in implementing the taps. State government action that discriminates against aliens is subject to strict scrutiny.

Further, the government must implement an alternative method of meeting its objective that is less burdensome on the protected rights of all aliens.

The F.B.I. could furnish the proper authority with substantiated evidence of any person, alien or citizen, suspected of subversive activity after which it could obtain a warrant authorizing taps over a specified period of time. This is an alternative to tapping the telephones indiscriminately without a search warrant. It is also less burdensome on the rights of all persons involved.

The order should be struck down as violative of the Equal Protection Clause.

First Amendment - Freedom of Speech

First Amendment freedom of speech is a preferred right under the United States Constitution, applicable to the states through the Fourteenth Amendment. It is not an absolute right and can be restricted by the government under certain situations.

All persons communicating with aliens suspected of espionage or subversive activity by the F.B.I. are subject to warrantless wiretaps. Such broad monitoring powers have a chilling effect on free speech, a preferred right under the First Amendment. It stifles what parties to telephone conversations want to discuss, legal or illegal.

The government would counter that the right to free speech is not absolute. Suspected espionage or subversion by foreign powers are proper grounds for restrictions by the government on telephone conversations involving aliens.

Nevertheless, protecting an individual's free and unregulated telephone speech balanced against unfettered telephone wiretapping in cases of suspected espionage and subversion clearly weighs in favor of protecting speech. A mere suspicion does not create a compelling state interest sufficient to override the chilling effect that results on free speech.

The executive order violates the free speech protections guaranteed under the First Amendment.

Overbreadth

An overbroad law is one that regulates a substantial amount of constitutionally protected expression as well as expression that is not constitutionally protected.

The executive order permits warrantless F.B.I. wiretaps of any alien suspected of espionage or subversive activity. These listening devices act to regulate not only conversations dealing with espionage and subversion but also any other conversations by aliens and citizens alike. The facts indicate that Jones sought to show at the trial that the F.B.I. had tapped telephones of United States citizens. Because the executive order allows regulation of both protected and unprotected expression, it is overbroad.

The order is overbroad and, therefore, void.

Executive Privilege

Although not expressly mentioned in the Constitution, an executive privilege is recognized to protect against the disclosure of presidential communications made in the exercise of executive power. The privilege affords the executive implied immunity where there is a compelling national interest to be protected.

Jones caused an F.B.I. agent to be subpoenaed to testify and produce records of the telephone taps in issue. The President claimed executive privilege for the F.B.I. agent who had been subpoenaed. The President will assert that the agent's testimony and the requested documents deal with espionage and subversion, matters of national security. His testimony is impliedly immune from discovery by way of the executive privilege. Also, such communications are of compelling national interest. Thus, the F.B.I. agent does not have to appear to testify or produce the records.

However, the wiretap issue involves only cases of suspected espionage. This is only a questionable national security risk. In such cases, the federal court may make an in-camera inspection of all relevant information and communications so that it can scrupulously protect against the disclosure of materials not found relevant while deciding what information is relevant to the rights that are allegedly being violated. Absent something more than a "suspicion" of a national security risk, the agent and his records are not protected by the immunity of the executive privilege. He must appear and provide his records for court inspection.

No executive privilege exists.

CONSTITUTIONAL LAW QUESTION #3

MOTHER v. SUBURBAN

Suburban Primary School ("Suburban") is a public school supported entirely by local property taxes and federal grants. The Parent-Teachers Association ("PTA") is an unincorporated association consisting of parents of some students at Suburban. PTA decided to institute an extracurricular program for the school's students, in which PTA would sponsor four courses, each to be held once a week, on school premises, after regular hours. Certain PTA members would voluntarily serve as teachers for the courses. After such classes, participating students would be allowed to take the "late" school bus home. The Suburban principal has agreed to let PTA use the school premises and bus for the program.

PTA determined that because of possible behavior problems, none of the courses would be co-educational.

Each parent was to register his child in person at 8:45 am. on the opening day of the program, and classes were to be filled on a "first-come, first-served" basis. Before the program began, it was described in a pamphlet given to each child attending Suburban to take home. The available courses were described as:

1. Embroidery - 8 girls, 5th and 6th grades, $3.00;
2. Creative Crafts - 10 boys, 2nd grade, $4.00;
3. Baseball Practice - 10 boys, 5th and 6th grades, $2.00;
4. Bible Studies - 12 girls, no fee.

Mother (M), who is not a PTA member, did not arrive at school on the opening day until 9:15 a.m. because of a flat tire on her car. M attempted to enroll her son Harold (H), a second grader at Suburban, in creative crafts, but was told that the course was filled. She also tried to enroll her daughter Alice (A), a sixth-grader at Suburban, in Baseball Practice, but was refused although several vacancies were left.

M has sued to compel enrollment of H in Creative Crafts, and of A in Baseball Practice. Two other parents, who are not members of PTA but who are taxpayers residing in the school district with children attending Suburban, have sued to enjoin continuation of the entire program. Both suits rely exclusively on rights guaranteed by or secured to the plaintiffs under the United States Constitution.

Assume that all proper defendants have been joined in both actions.

What constitutional issues are raised by the suits, and how should they be decided? Discuss.

IRAC OUTLINE SHEET

(I)	(R)	(A)	(C)

EXAMPLE OF PROPER IRAC OUTLINE

MOTHER'S (M'S) SUIT TO COMPEL ALICE'S (A'S) ENROLLMENT IN BASEBALL:

(I)	(R)	(A)	(C)
THIRD PARTY STANDING	Claimant May Assert Rights Of Third Party	M mother of H M sued Suburban (S) to compel H's enrollment in creative crafts M told course filled	Standing
	Difficult/Impossible Assert Own Rights	H a second grader	
PROCEDURAL DUE PROCESS	Property Right	Enrollment in creative crafts (education)	No Violation
	Notice/Opportunity Heard	Each parent was to register his child at 8:45 a.m. on opening day of the program First-come first-served basis Before program began, it was described in pamphlet given to each child to take home Available classes described M did not arrive at school until 9:15 a.m./flat tire/course filled	

MOTHER'S (M'S) SUIT TO COMPEL ALICE'S (A'S) ENROLLMENT IN BASEBALL:

(I)	(R)	(A)	(C)
THIRD PARTY STANDING	Claimant May Assert	M mother of A	Standing
	Rights Of Third Party	M sued to compel A's enrollment in baseball Several vacancies left	
	Difficult/Impossible Assert Own Rights	A sixth grader	
EQUAL PROTECTION	Government Regulation	PTA unincorporated association consisting of parents of some students at S S is public school supported entirely by local property taxes & federal grants	Equal Protection Violation
	Discriminate	Baseball practice-10 boys only	
	Arbitrary Classification	No courses co-educational	
	Individuals Similarly Situated	Baseball class Boys only	
STATE ACTION	Nexus Test	S public school supported by local taxes, federal grants supra PTA unincorporated association supra PTA decided to institute extracurricular program for students, each once a week on school premises after regular hours Certain PTA members would voluntarily serve as teachers for courses After classes, participating students allowed to take "late" school bus home S principal agreed to let PTA use school premises & bus for program Pamphlet given to each child attending S	State Action
INTENTIONAL DISCRIMINATION	Discriminatory Purpose	Not co-educational Baseball practice-10 boys	De Jure Discrimination
CLASSIFY DISCRIMINATION	Gender-Quasi Suspect	A refused enrollment although several vacancies were left	Violation
	Intermediate Scrutiny	Boys only (intentional gender discrimination)	
	Substantially Related Important Government Objective	PTA determined that "because possible behavior problems" no co-ed classes	

(I)	(R)	(A)	(C)
CLASSIFY DISCRIMINATION	Gender - Quasi Suspect	A refused enrollment although several vacancies were left	Violation
	Intermediate Scrutiny	Boys only (intentional gender discrimination)	
	Substantially Related Important Government Objective	PTA determined that "because possible behavior problems" no co-ed classes	

TWO PARENTS/TAXPAYERS' SUIT TO ENJOIN CONTINUATION OF PROGRAM:

(I)	(R)	(A)	(C)
MUNICIPAL TAXPAYER STANDING:	Municipal Taxpayer	Two other parents who are not members of PTA but are taxpayers residing in school district with children attending S have sued to enjoin program	Standing
	Measurable Expenditures	S program supported by local property taxes supra PTA instituted program supra	
FEDERAL TAXPAYER STANDING	Federal Taxpayer	Parents are taxpayers supra	Standing
	Federal Taxing/Spending Power	School supported by federal grants supra	
	Exceeds Constitutional Limitation	Federal grants supra Bible studies class/no fee	
FIRST AMENDMENT ESTABLISHMENT CLAUSE	Government Regulation	Public school program	Violation
	Secular Purpose	Bible studies course	
	Effect Neither Advances/Inhibits Religion	No fee Other courses had \$3-\$4 fee	
	No Excessive Entanglement	Supported entirely by local taxes/federal grants supra Bible studies no fee	
FIRST AMENDMENT FREE EXERCISE CLAUSE	Government Regulation	Supra	Violation
	Burden On Religion	Advance one religion over another	
	Non-Neutrality	Advance one religion over another	
	Compelling State Interest	Sponsoring Bible studies class?	

EXAMPLE OF IRAC CONSTITUTIONAL LAW ISSUE

(I) **Equal Protection**

(R) The Equal Protection Clause prohibits (1) government regulations that (2) discriminate on the basis of an (3) arbitrary classification as (4) individuals similarly situated must be treated the same.

(A) M will argue that Suburban is a public school supported entirely by local property taxes and federal grants. The PTA is a group consisting of parents of some Suburban students. Although it is an unincorporated association, the PTA enforces school policy making it an extension of the school. Thus, the program, instituted by the PTA and sanctioned by Suburban, which limits the baseball class to boys is akin to a (1) government regulation.

The program allows boys to play baseball but prevents girls from participating even though vacancies exist. The United States Supreme Court has ruled that gender based regulations treating girls differently are (2) discriminatory. Since the program is not co-educational, it creates an (3) arbitrary classification.

Further, girls at Suburban are not treated the same as boys (4) similarly situated at Suburban. Boys who want to play are permitted to enroll in baseball practice where vacancies exist but girls who want to play are not despite the same vacancies.

(C) Alice has raised a proper Equal Protection Clause challenge.

SUGGESTED MODEL ANSWER

MOTHER'S (M) SUIT TO COMPEL ENROLLMENT OF HAROLD IN CRAFTS CLASS:

Procedure - Third Party Standing

A claimant may assert the rights of a third party where the third party would find it difficult or impossible to vindicate his own rights.

M is Harold's mother. The mother/child relationship between the two allows M, as claimant, to assert Harold's constitutional rights. She has sued Suburban to compel Harold's enrollment in creative crafts. He was told that the class was filled and was, therefore, denied admission. Harold is the injured third party. However, Harold is only in the second grade. It would be difficult if not impossible to expect him to bring suit on his own behalf.

M has standing to bring suit on Harold's behalf.

Procedural Due Process

The United States Constitution guarantees that where a property right is involved, one must be given notice and an opportunity to be heard before being denied such a right.

M will assert that enrollment in the creative crafts class is an important educational opportunity for her son. As such, it is a valuable property right to which her child is entitled.

However, before the program began, each child at Suburban school was given a pamphlet to take home describing the available classes and the enrollment procedure. The pamphlet also stated that the classes would be filled on a first-come, first-served basis. Registration would begin at 8:45 a.m. on the opening day of class. The pamphlet gave sufficient notice concerning registration procedures.

Suburban will establish that M did not arrive at school until 9:15 a.m. This was 30 minutes after registration had begun. By the time she arrived, the class was filled. If M had been on time, she would have been able to register H in the class when openings were still available. Through no fault of Suburban, M had a flat tire on her way to school and missed her opportunity to be heard.

Therefore, there is no violation of Harold's procedural due process rights.

MOTHER'S (M'S) SUIT TO COMPEL ALICE'S (A'S) ENROLLMENT IN BASEBALL:

Procedure - Third Party Standing

Defined supra.

M is Alice's mother. The mother/child relationship between the two allows M, as claimant, to assert Alice's constitutional rights. She has sued Suburban to compel Alice's enrollment in baseball. Alice was denied enrollment although several vacancies were left. Alice is the injured third party. Yet, Alice is only in the sixth grade. It would be difficult if not impossible to expect Alice to bring suit on her own behalf.

Mother has standing to bring suit on Alice's behalf.

Equal Protection

The Equal Protection Clause prohibits government regulations that discriminate on the basis of an arbitrary classification as individuals similarly situated must be treated the same.

Suburban is a public school supported entirely by local property taxes and federal grants. The PTA is a group consisting of parents of some Suburban students. Although it is an unincorporated association, the PTA enforces school policy making it an extension of the school. Thus, the program, instituted by the PTA and sanctioned by Suburban, which limits the baseball class to boys is akin to a government regulation.

The program allows boys to play baseball but prevents girls from participating even though vacancies exist. The United States Supreme Court has ruled that gender based regulations treating girls differently are discriminatory. Since the program is not co-educational, it creates an arbitrary classification.

Further, girls at Suburban are not treated the same as boys similarly situated at Suburban. Boys who want to play are permitted to enroll in baseball practice where vacancies exist but girls who want to play are not despite the same vacancies.

Alice has raised a proper Equal Protection Clause challenge.

State Action

In order to establish a violation of Equal Protection Clause, a nexus must be shown between the alleged discriminatory activity and the state's involvement.

Suburban is a public school entirely supported by local taxes and federal grants. The PTA, an unincorporated association, has instituted the extra-curricular program once a week on school premises after regular hours. The use of public taxes to support these activities demonstrates a significant relationship commonly referred to as a nexus between the state run school district and the program.

The PTA will contend that the program is extracurricular. The PTA members who serve as teachers do so on a voluntary basis. No tax money is being used to run the program thereby negating a nexus between the school and the program.

Still, the programs are being taught on school premises. After classes, participating students are allowed to take the "late" school bus home. The Suburban principal has agreed to let the PTA use the school premises and has authorized the use of school time and resources to distribute pamphlets to each school child. These facts demonstrate the clear, direct and significant involvement of Suburban school with the program.

State action is present.

Intentional Discrimination

Where a government action has a discriminatory purpose, de jure discrimination may be found.

The PTA baseball class is not co-educational. Instead it is restricted to ten boys only. Such a restriction, by its terms, has a intentional discriminatory purpose.

Therefore, de jure discrimination will be found.

Classification Of The Discrimination

Gender based discrimination is considered a quasi-suspect classification. Intermediate scrutiny is applied to a government regulation which intentionally discriminates on the basis of gender. The regulation will violate the Equal Protection Clause unless it is substantially related to an important governmental objective.

Alice was refused enrollment in the baseball class although several vacancies were left. The refusal was solely because she is a girl. The PTA has created gender based discrimination, a quasi suspect classification. Intermediate scrutiny will be applied to the PTA regulation as it intentionally discriminates solely on the basis of gender.

The PTA determined that because of possible behavior problems, the classes should not be coeducational. However, this appears to be an administrative decision. Student behavior problems can be controlled by discipline and supervision. Student discipline in elementary school baseball class does not appear to be so substantially related to an important governmental objective that it justifies exclusion of girls from baseball.

Suburban has engaged in discriminatory activities that violate the Equal Protection Clause of the United States Constitution. Alice should be enrolled in the baseball class.

TWO PARENTS/TAXPAYERS' SUIT TO ENJOIN CONTINUATION OF PROGRAM:

Procedure - Municipal Taxpayer Standing

A municipal taxpayer may bring suit if he can establish measurable state expenditures associated with the program to which he is objecting.

The facts indicate that two other parents, who are not members of the PTA but are taxpayers residing in the school district with children attending Suburban school, have sued to enjoin the program. As municipal taxpayers, they will assert that Suburban school is supported by their local property taxes. The amount of money required to support this extra-curricular program on school premises is a measurable state expenditure.

It appears that the parents may have municipal taxpayer standing to bring suit.

Procedural - Federal Taxpayer Standing

A federal taxpayer may have standing to bring suit if the challenged federal action arises from the taxing and spending power and it exceeds a specific constitutional limitation on the taxing and spending power.

The two parents reside in the school district and are apparently federal taxpayers. Since the Suburban school is supported by federal grants, they are objecting to a program supported by their federal taxes.

There are no facts indicating that the federal grants given to Suburban school are specifically earmarked for any particular program or expenditure. Thus, the federal funds are, in part, funding the school's participation in the extra-curricular programs.

These funds are entirely funding the Bible studies class that requires no fee for student participation. The parents are alleging that the Bible studies class violates both the First Amendment Establishment Clause and Free Exercise Clause. It appears that the expenditures exceed a specific First Amendment constitutional limitation designed to bar taxation and spending for the support of religion.

The parents have federal taxpayer standing to bring suit.

First Amendment - Freedom Of Religion - The Establishment Clause

The First Amendment, applicable to the states through the Fourteenth Amendment, prohibits the establishment of a religion by government entities. A valid government regulation must have a secular purpose, effect that neither advances nor inhibits religion and there must not be excessive governmental entanglement.

The taxpayers will contend that the Bible studies class promotes religious belief and faith. The purpose of the class is religious, not secular.

The school may rebut that the purpose of the class is to study the historical importance of biblical events. However, there are insufficient facts to make this determination. The class, therefore, seems to be religious in nature.

No fee is charged for the Bible studies class. There is a $2-$4 fee for all of the other classes. Therefore, the school appears to be giving extra support to the Bible studies class. The effect of this extra support is to encourage students to attend a free class at the exclusion of other classes for which students must pay. The effect is to advance the religious views taught in Bible studies.

The Bible studies class is supported entirely by the local taxes and federal grants. The taxpayers will assert that the use of public funds to support a program that encourages religion demonstrates excessive governmental entanglement.

It appears that the Bible studies class violates the Establishment Clause of the First Amendment and should be enjoined.

First Amendment - Free Exercise Clause

The First Amendment, applicable to the states through the Fourteenth Amendment, prohibits a government regulation which interferes with the free exercise of religion. In determining the validity of the government regulation, the court will look to the burden on religion, non-neutrality of the law, and whether a compelling state interest exists to uphold the regulation.

The taxpayers will assert that the action of the school equates to state promotion of Bible studies. This is a form of government regulation. The bible studies class advances Christian religion over other religions that do not recognize the Bible.

A program that discriminates in favor of one religion interferes with the free exercise of those who choose a different belief system. The program directly burdens religion and is non-neutral. There appears to be no compelling state interest in sponsoring a Bible studies class.

Therefore, the Bible studies class violates the Free Exercise Clause of the First Amendment.

Remedy

The court will order all unconstitutional parts of the program to be severed. In this case, the gender classifications will be deleted from the program and the Bible studies class should be enjoined immediately.

CONSTITUTIONAL LAW QUESTION #4

CHURCH v. CITY

On October 3, 1977, City adopted a municipal ordinance prohibiting the placing of "commercial" signs on rooftops within city limits, with the stated purpose of improving the quality of life within City by emphasizing and protecting aesthetic values." The ordinance also provided that all signs in place on the date of its adoption, in violation of its terms, must be removed within five years of that date.

In September, 1979, Rugged Cross Church (Church), with its church building situated within City's limits, placed a 20-foot blue neon-lighted sign in the shape of a cross on its church roof, with the message "Join and Support Our Church" in white neon rights inside the blue neon borders of the cross.

After the Church sign was in place, various citizens of City urged that the City sign ordinance be amended to include all rooftop signs in City. Other citizens complained to City officials that Church's sign was "an eyesore."

Effective October 1, 1979, City amended its sign ordinance by deleting the word "commercial." City then notified Church that its entire neon rooftop sign would have to be removed within five years.

Church has brought suit against City in a state trial court of proper jurisdiction, claiming that the amended City sign ordinance is invalid under the United States Constitution, both (1) by its terms and general application, and (2) as City seeks to apply it to Church.

How should the court rule on each of Church's claims? Discuss.

IRAC OUTLINE SHEET

(I)	(R)	(A)	(C)

EXAMPLE OF PROPER IRAC OUTLINE

CHURCH v. CITY (C)

1.(A) VALIDITY OF AMENDED ORDINANCE - BY ITS TERMS

(I)	(R)	(A)	(C)
ZONING-10TH AMENDMENT	Police Powers	On 10/3/77 C adopted a municipal ordinance prohibiting placing commercial signs on rooftops in City with the stated purpose of improving quality of life by emphasizing & protecting aesthetic values (safety, welfare, environment) Effective 10/1/79, C amended its sign ordinance by deleting commercial	Valid Zoning
NON-CONFORMING USE	A Use In Existence When Ordinance Passed	9/79 Church placed 20' sign on its rooftop 10/3/77 ordinance 10/1/79 amended ordinance passed	
	Reasonable Time Amortization	C notified Church that its sign would have to be removed within 5 years	
COMPREHENSIVE PLAN	Applies To All Similarly Situated	10/1/79 amended ordinance prohibits placing of all signs on rooftops within city limits supra	Comprehensive Plan
VARIANCE	Restrictions Cause Unnecessary Hardship	In 9/79 Church with its building situated within C limits, placed 20-ft. blue neon sign in the shape of a cross on its roof 10/1/79 ordinance prohibits rooftop signs in city supra C notified church that its entire neon rooftop sign would have to be removed within 5 years	No Variance

1.(B) VALIDITY OF AMENDED ORDINANCE - BY GENERAL APPLICATION

(I)	(R)	(A)	(C)
FIRST AMENDMENT FREE SPEECH	Government Regulation	10/1/79 ordinance prohibits signs on rooftops in City Ordinance prohibits signs on rooftops supra	No First Amendment Violation
	Time/PlaceManner Permitted:	Sign reads Join-Support our Church	
	Content Neutral	Message "Join & support"	
	Narrowly Tailored	Ordinance supra	
	Serve Significant Interest	Purpose = improve quality of life & protect aaesthetic values	
	Alternative Channels	Ordinance applies to rooftop signs only	

2. VALIDITY OF AMENDED ORDINANCE BY APPLICATION TO CHURCH

(I)	(R)	(A)	(C)
FIRST AMENDMENT FREE EXERCISE CLAUSE	Government Regulation	10/1/79 ordinance supra	No First Amendment Violation
	Burden On Religion	20 foot neon sign in shape of cross on roof/message join & support our church in white neon/eyesore	
	Non-Neutrality	City requiring removal of Church sign	
	Compelling State Interest	Purpose in improve quality of life supra	
EQUAL PROTECTION	Government Regulation	Supra	No Equal Protection Violation
	Discriminate	Rooftop signs	
	Arbitrary Classification	No facts	
	Individuals Similarly Situated	No facts	

EXAMPLE OF IRAC CONSTITUTIONAL LAW ISSUE

(I) **First Amendment - Free Exercise Clause**

(R) The First Amendment, applicable to the states through the Fourteenth Amendment, prohibits (1) a government regulation which interferes with the free exercise of religion. In determining the validity of government regulation, the court will look to (2) the burden on religion, (3) non-neutrality of the law, and (4) whether a compelling state interest exists to uphold the regulation.

(A) The Church will argue that the City ordinance in question equates to (1) a government regulation. Further, the 20-foot high rooftop sign in the shape of a cross is an expression of its religious belief. Any regulation that requires the removal of the sign (2) substantially burdens the exercise of its religious belief. The sign's message "Join and Support our Church" encourages others to join the Church and exercise the same belief. By requiring removal of the sign, City is preventing the growth and dissemination of Church's religion and its religious belief, as such, it is (3) a non-neutral regulation. This acts to prohibit Church's free exercise of religious belief.

Nevertheless, the placement of the cross on the Church rooftop is not necessary to the practice of Church's religious belief. While the cross on the roof may attract new members to the Church, there are no facts indicating that placement of the cross is an integral part of the religion's belief or its practice. Church may still disseminate its message and exercise its religious belief if the cross is located elsewhere by merely relocating the sign. Thus, the burden is minor. Moreover, because the amended ordinance applies to all signs, the ordinance is neutral in its application. Finally, (4) the state's interest to improve the quality of life and protect aesthetic values against eyesores, appears to be compelling.

(C) It appears that the ordinance does not violate the Free Exercise Clause of the First Amendment.

SUGGESTED MODEL ANSWER

CHURCH v. CITY

1.(A) VALIDITY OF AMENDED CITY ORDINANCE BY ITS TERMS:

Zoning - Tenth Amendment

The Tenth Amendment of the United States Constitution reserves to the states through its police powers the right to regulate the health, safety, welfare, environment, aesthetics, and morals of its citizens.

On 10/3/77, City adopted a municipal ordinance prohibiting commercial rooftop signs in City. It was enacted with the stated purpose of improving the quality of life by emphasizing and protecting aesthetic values within the City limits. Rooftop signs are considered eyesores by many citizens. They impact on the aesthetic quality of City's local environment. Rooftop signs could create both a distraction to motorists and a danger to pedestrians below them if not properly maintained. The local concern regarding safety, citizen welfare, and environment would be impacted. The City's purpose in adopting the ordinance clearly falls within acceptable police powers reserved to the state through the Tenth Amendment.

When the ordinance was amended to be effective 10/l/79, the single word "commercial" was deleted. The identical purpose established above was present. For the same reason, the amended ordinance was a proper exercise of the state's police powers under the Tenth Amendment.

Non-Conforming Use

A non-conforming use is a use in existence when the zoning ordinance is passed which is not permitted in the zone where the property is located. The ordinance must allow a reasonable time for amortization of the non-conforming use.

The Church will assert that its 20 foot blue neon sign was erected in September 1979. The cross was not commercial in nature and was, therefore, in conformity with the original 10/3/77 ordinance. Since its use was in existence prior to passage of the 10/l/79 amended ordinance and was only made non-conforming because of the amendment, the sign should be allowed to remain.

However, the amended ordinance provides that all rooftop signs in place at the time of the adoption of the ordinance "be removed within five years." Church was notified that its neon sign would have to be removed. The five-year period allowed for removal is a reasonable time for the Church to amortize its investment before it must take the sign down or relocate it.

The ordinance has reasonably provided for non-conforming uses.

Comprehensive Plan

A zoning plan, to be valid, must be comprehensive and apply to all landowners similarly situated.

The purpose of the ordinance is to improve the quality of life for City citizens. The ordinance provides for this public need which is best served by such a restriction and is comprehensive in its application.

The City ordinance, as amended, restricts all rooftop signs in the City. Since it applies equally to all landowners/occupiers similarly situated in City who have rooftop signs on their buildings, it does not discriminate.

Therefore, the ordinance is a comprehensive plan.

Variance

A valid zoning plan requires a variance for non-conforming uses in existence at the time of the ordinance to permit relief where the restrictions contained in the ordinance cause the owner practical difficulty or unnecessary hardship.

Church will contend that it erected a 20-foot blue neon lighted sign in the shape of a cross on its roof in September 1979, prior to the date of the amended ordinance. It did so because of its need to reach City citizens through the message on its sign, a message that is integral to its practice of religion. If the sign is removed from the rooftop due to City's restrictions, it would be more difficult to attract the attention of potential followers creating a practical difficulty in reaching these individuals. Such unique circumstances demonstrate an unnecessary hardship on the Church congregation.

Yet, Church's hardship appears to be self-created. Its ability to get its message to City citizens is not limited to its use of rooftop signs. There are numerous other modes of available communication, including the relocation of the sign anywhere else on the Church's premises. The requirement that Church relocate its sign appears to be more of an inconvenience rather than a practical difficulty or unnecessary hardship. The five years given by the ordinance to bring the location of the sign into compliance appears more than reasonable in order for Church to receive a reasonable return on its existing sign.

Thus, relief from the sign restriction should not be extended beyond the five year period. The variance will not be allowed as prescribed by the ordinance.

The amended ordinance is valid by its terms.

1.(B) VALIDITY OF THE ORDINANCE BY GENERAL APPLICATION:

First Amendment - Speech

The First Amendment, applicable to the states through the Fourteenth Amendment, protects freedom of speech. The government may regulate conduct based on time, place and manner but restrictions must be content neutral, narrowly tailored, serve a significant government interest and alternative channels of communication must exist.

The Church will assert that the 10/1/79 ordinance that prohibits it from displaying the neon cross on its rooftop with the message "Join and Support our Church," unlawfully restricts Church's right to communicate with prospective religious members. The sign is necessary to attract attention and convey Church's message. The government ordinance regulates the content of Church's message, a violation of free speech.

However, City will point out that the ordinance only regulates the conduct of its citizens concerning placement of signs on their rooftops. The ordinance does not regulate the messages contained in the signs. The ordinance does not seek to outlaw the contents of communication. It only restricts places where signs may or may not be located.

Moreover, Church may post its cross with its above-stated message anywhere other than on its rooftop. Thus, the ordinance relates to the place and manner in which signs, both commercial and noncommercial, may be erected. It is neutral as to the content of the sign.

Further, since the regulation does not burden substantially more speech than necessary to further

City's interest in aesthetics, it is narrowly tailored.

City's interests in emphasizing, protecting, and improving the quality of life for its citizens is a significant government interest.

Finally, as stated above, Church may post its message anywhere other than its rooftop. Therefore, alternative channels of communication exist.

Since recent case law does permit ordinances to regulate in this manner, the ordinance is not an infringement on free speech.

Based on the foregoing, the amended ordinance is valid in its general application.

2. VALIDITY OF AMENDED CITY ORDINANCE AS IT APPLES TO CHURCH:

First Amendment - Free Exercise Clause

The First Amendment, applicable to the states through the Fourteenth Amendment, prohibits a government regulation which interferes with the free exercise of religion. In determining the validity of government regulation, the court will look to the burden on religion, non-neutrality of the law, and whether a compelling state interest exists to uphold the regulation.

The Church will argue that the City ordinance in question equates to a government regulation. Further, the 20-foot high rooftop sign in the shape of a cross is an expression of its religious belief. Any regulation that requires the removal of the sign substantially burdens the exercise of its religious belief.

The sign's message "Join and Support our Church" encourages others to join the Church and exercise the same belief. By requiring removal of the sign, City is preventing the growth and dissemination of Church's religion and its religious belief, as such, it is a non-neutral regulation. This acts to prohibit Church's free exercise of religious belief.

Nevertheless, the placement of the cross on the Church rooftop is not necessary to the practice of Church's religious belief. While the cross on the roof may attract new members to the Church, there are no facts indicating that placement of the cross is an integral part of the religion's belief or its practice. Church may still disseminate its message and exercise its religious belief if the cross is located elsewhere by merely relocating the sign. Thus, the burden is minor.

Moreover, because the amended ordinance applies to all signs, the ordinance is neutral in its application. Finally, the state's interest to improve the quality of life and protect aesthetic values against eyesores, appears to be compelling.

It appears that the ordinance does not violate the Free Exercise Clause of the First Amendment.

Equal Protection

The Equal Protection Clause prohibits government regulations that discriminate on the basis of an arbitrary classification as individuals similarly situated must be treated the same.

The Church will contend that the City ordinance represents a government regulation. The effect of the ordinance is that it discriminates against Church and all other rooftop sign owners.

However, the ordinance applies to all rooftop signs within the city limits. It does not discriminate against any individual or class of persons. Further, since the ordinance is content and impact neutral (supra), the Church cannot establish an arbitrary classification. Since it is not being treated differently than other rooftop sign owners similarly situated, Church cannot prevail.

The ordinance does not violate the Equal Protection Clause.

CONSTITUTIONAL LAW QUESTION #5

MAYO TAXPAYERS v. CHURCH

The Mayo Christian Church (Church) is located in the city of Mayo, State X. The governing body of Church established the Lawyers Society (Society) as a State X nonprofit corporation, to increase the participation of Church in Mayo's community problems. Society is composed exclusively of Church members who are lawyers licensed to practice in State X, all of whom have agreed to work for Society without compensation. Society offers free legal services by its lawyer members to residents of Mayo who are "victims of racial or religious discrimination." Society is financially supported both by Church funds and by a grant of funds from Agency, which administers a State X program providing public funds to legal aid organizations.

Soon after its establishment, Society "targeted" certain apparent instances of discrimination in Mayo as appropriate objectives for its services. Society members have directly approached various Mayo residents who appeared to be victims of discrimination, met with them, explained their legal rights, and then offered them free legal assistance in commencing litigation in State X courts aimed at redressing the apparent instances of discrimination.

However, Society has begun to have legal problems of its own:

a. An organization called "Mayo Taxpayers for Separation of Church and State" (Taxpayers), consisting of State X taxpayers who are residents of Mayo, has brought an action in federal court in State X against Church, Society, and Agency. The complaint challenges the propriety of the use of public funds by a Church, Society, and Agency. The complaint challenges the propriety of the use of public funds by a church-sponsored organization and seeks a judgment prohibiting Agency from granting funds to Society.

b. Jay, a lawyer admitted to practice in State X, volunteered to join and work for Society without compensation. He was rejected because he was not a Church member. Jay has brought an action in federal court in State X against Church, Society, and Agency, seeking a judgment requiring Society to admit him to membership. He alleges that his exclusion from membership in Society as an organization supported by public funds constitutes an unlawful discrimination in violation of the United States Constitution.

c. The State X Bar Association (Bar), which is responsible for the enforcement of State X law regulating the practice of law, has charged that the solicitation practices of Society's members violate the State X attorneys' professional disciplinary code, which prohibits "direct solicitation" of clients and legal work by lawyers. Bar has instituted an action in State X court against Society and its members, seeking an injunction prohibiting any further "solicitation" activity by Society members.

What issues arising under the United States Constitution are involved in these three cases, and how should each issue be decided? Discuss.

IRAC OUTLINE SHEET

(I)	(R)	(A)	(C)

EXAMPLE OF PROPER IRAC OUTLINE

A. MAYO TAXPAYERS v. CHURCH (C), SOCIETY (S) and AGENCY (A)

(I)	(R)	(A)	(C)
ASSOCIATION STANDING	Members Have Standing	An organization called "Mayo Taxpayers for separation of Church & consisting of State X taxpayers who are residents of Mayo, has brought an action in the federal court in State X against C,S, &A The complaint challenges the propriety of the use of public funds by a C,S, & A & the use of public funds by a church sponsored organization	Proper Standing
	Interest Relevant To Association's Purpose	S is financially supported both by C funds & a grant from A A administers a State X program providing public funds to legal aid organizations	
	Members Not Indispensable Parties	Taxpayers seek a judgment prohibiting A from granting funds to S Individual participation not necessary	
FIRST AMENDMENT ESTABLISHMENT CLAUSE	Government Regulation	Society, a C established society offering free legal services to residents of Mayo who are "victims" of racial or religious discrimination S is financially supported both by C funds & by a grant of funds from A, which administers a State X program providing public funds to legal aid organizations	No Violation
	Secular Purpose	The governing body of C established S as a State X nonprofit organization to increase the participation of C in Mayo's community problems S offers free legal services by its lawyer members to residents of Mayo who are "victims of racial or religious discrimination"	
	Effect Neither Advances/ Inhibits Religion	S established to increase the participation of C in Mayo's community problems S offers free legal services to residents of Mayo who are "victims" supra Soon after its establishment, S "targeted" certain apparent instances of discrimination in Mayo as appropriate objectives for its services S members have directly approached various Mayo residents who appeared to be victims of discrimination, met with them explained their legal rights, & offered them free legal assistance in commencing litigation in State X courts aimed at redressing the apparent instances of discrimination	
	No Excessive Entanglement	S is financially supported both by C funds & by a grant of funds from A	

B. JAY v. CHURCH (C), SOCIETY (S) & AGENCY (A)

(I)	(R)	(A)	(C)
EQUAL PROTECTION	Government Regulation	S is financially supported by C & A supra S is composed exclusively of C members who are licensed to practice in State X S is a State X, nonprofit corporation that offers free legal services to residents of Mayo who are victims" supra	Possible Violation
	Discriminate	J, a lawyer admitted to practice in State X volunteered to join & work for S without compensation He was rejected because he was not a C member	

(I)	(R)	(A)	(C)
	Arbitrary Classification	C members only	
	Individuals Similarly Situated	S is composed exclusively of C members who are licensed to practice in State X J rejected because he was not a C member	
STATE ACTION	Nexus Test	S is financially supported both by C funds & by a grant of funds from A, supra	State Action
CLASSIFY DISCRIMINATION	Fundamental Right	J, a lawyer admitted to practice was rejected because not a Church member	Violation
	Strict Scrutiny	S's policy of exclusion based on religion	
	Compelling State Interest	(valid administrative decision?)	
	Least Burdensome Alternative	Qualifying test for all members	

C. STATE BAR (B) v. SOCIETY (S)

(I)	(R)	(A)	(C)
FIRST AMENDMENT FREE SPEECH	Preferred Right	B, which is responsible for the enforcement of State X law regulating the practice of law has charged that the solicitation practices of S's members violate the State's professional disciplinary code, which prohibits "direct solicitation" of clients & legal work by lawyers S nonprofit, supra S approached "victims" & offered free legal assistance, supra	Violation
	Not Absolute	B regulates practice of law	
OVERBREADTH	Regulation Of Protected & Unprotected Expression	B has instituted an action in State X court against & its members, seeking an injunction prohibiting any further "solicitation" activity by S members	Overbroad
VAGUENESS	Statute - No Notice	B has instituted an action, supra, prohibiting "solicitation"	Vague
	Reasonable Person	S lawyers	
FIRST AMENDMENT FREEDOM OF ASSOCIATION	Association Without Undue Governmental Restraint	B has instituted an action prohibiting "solicitation" supra S members have directly approached victims" supra	Violation

EXAMPLE OF IRAC CONSTITUTIONAL LAW ISSUE

(I) **First Amendment - Freedom of Religion - Establishment Clause**

(R) The First Amendment, applicable to the states through the Fourteenth Amendment, prohibits the establishment of a religion by government entities. A (1) valid government regulation must have a (2) secular purpose, (3) effect that neither advances nor inhibits religion and there must not be (4) excessive governmental entanglement.

(A) Society is a church established organization offering free legal services to residents of Mayo who are victims of racial or religious discrimination.

Society is financially supported both by Church funds and by a grant of funds from Agency. Agency, in its capacity as a government entity, administers a State X program which provides public funds to legal aid organizations. The allocation of public funds to Society by this government agency demonstrates a close nexus between public funds and their alleged use to support a religious activity. The criteria upon which Agency grants the funds to Society would be deemed a (1) government regulation.

Public funds are being provided to support the Church-sponsored Society. The governing body of Church established Society as a non-profit organization to increase participation of Church members in Mayo's community problems. Society offers free legal services by its lawyer members to residents of Mayo who are victims of racial or religious discrimination. Because the purpose of Society is to redress discrimination rather than to promote religious beliefs, Society's activities are (2) secular in nature.

Society was established to increase the participation of Church members in Mayo's community problems. It offers free legal services by its lawyer members to all residents of Mayo who have been victims of racial or religious discrimination. Soon after its establishment, Society "targeted" certain apparent instances of discrimination in Mayo as appropriate objectives of its services. Society members have directly approached various Mayo residents who appeared to be victims of discrimination. Whether or not these victims are Church members has no bearing on Society's willingness to approach, meet with, explain or offer to represent them. Therefore, Society is not (3) advancing or inhibiting religion through its activities. Instead, Society is assisting Mayo citizens in their fight to redress apparent instances of racial and religious discrimination in their community, irrespective of what race, religion or creed to which the individual victim subscribes.

Taxpayers will counter that public funds are being used to redress discrimination that specifically involves religion. By doing so, religion is directly benefiting from the use of public funds spent on its behalf. The support to a Church-sponsored organization like Society both aids and advances religious views.

However, Society is not sponsoring religion by helping victims of racial or religious discrimination. It is merely offering free legal assistance by commencing litigation in State X courts with an eye towards redressing the apparent instances of discrimination. The effect of these efforts is to advance equality in the Mayo community rather than to aid or advance religion.

Society is financially supported partially by a grant of funds from Agency, which administers a State X program providing funds to legal aid organizations. The funding is an administrative function and appears to involve no further involvement. There is no indication that Agency must actively supervise the activities of Society to ensure that the funds are being used for legal services. Further, Society is not totally funded by Agency. Church funds are also being used to fund Society's non-profit legal representation. Therefore, there appears to be no (4) excessive government entanglement between the funds provided to Society by Agency.

(C) The Taxpayers will be unsuccessful in their First Amendment Establishment Clause challenge and should be denied a judgment prohibiting Agency from granting funds to Society.

SUGGESTED MODEL ANSWER

A. MAYO TAXPAYERS v. CHURCH, SOCIETY AND AGENCY

Procedure - Association Standing

Associations have standing to assert the rights of their members where the members themselves would have standing, the interest asserted is relevant to the association's purpose and the members themselves are not indispensable parties.

An organization called "Mayo Taxpayers for Separation of Church and State" consisting of State X taxpayers who are residents of Mayo, has brought an action in State X federal court against Church, Society and Agency. The complaint challenges the propriety of the use of public funds by Church, Society, and Agency.

Taxpayers represent state taxpayers claiming injury. Thus, Taxpayers have standing to file their complaint challenging the propriety of the use of public funds by a church-sponsored organization because there is an injury in fact to its members.

Society is financially supported both by Church funds and by a grant of funds from Agency. Agency administers a State X program providing public funds to legal aid organizations. Taxpayers will argue that their state taxes are being used to support Society in its Church related activities. Thus, the interest asserted is directly relevant to the association's purpose of separating Church and State.

Further, the relief sought is a judgment prohibiting Agency from granting funds to Society. Such relief does not require participation of the individual members of Taxpayers. Therefore, the members themselves are not indispensable parties.

The Mayo Taxpayers have standing to sue.

First Amendment - Freedom of Religion - The Establishment Clause

The First Amendment, applicable to the states through the Fourteenth Amendment, prohibits the establishment of a religion by government entities. A valid government regulation must have a secular purpose, an effect that neither advances nor inhibits religion and there must not be excessive governmental entanglement.

Society is a church established organization offering free legal services to residents of Mayo who are victims of racial or religious discrimination. Society is financially supported both by Church funds and by a grant of funds from Agency. Agency, in its capacity as a government entity, administers a State X program which provides public funds to legal aid organizations. The allocation of public funds to Society by this government agency demonstrates a close nexus between public funds and their alleged use to support a religious activity. The criteria upon which Agency grants the funds to Society is deemed a government regulation.

Public funds are being provided to support the Church-sponsored Society. The governing body of Church established Society as a non-profit organization to increase participation of Church members in Mayo's community problems. Society offers free legal services by its lawyer members to residents of Mayo who are victims of racial or religious discrimination. Because the purpose of Society is to redress discrimination rather than to promote religious beliefs, Society's activities are secular in nature.

Society was established to increase the participation of Church members in Mayo's community problems. It offers free legal services by its lawyer members to all residents of Mayo who have been victims of racial or religious discrimination. Soon after its establishment, Society "targeted" certain apparent instances of discrimination in Mayo as appropriate objectives of its services. Society members have directly approached various Mayo residents who appeared to be victims of discrimination. Whether or not these victims are Church members has no bearing on Society's willingness to approach, meet with, explain or offer to represent them. Therefore, Society is neither advancing nor inhibiting religion through its activities. Instead, Society is assisting Mayo citizens in their fight to redress apparent instances of racial and religious discrimination in their community, irrespective of what race, religion or creed to which the individual victim subscribes.

Taxpayers will counter that public funds are being used to redress discrimination that specifically involves religion. By doing so, religion is directly benefiting from the use of public funds spent on its behalf. The support to a Church-sponsored organization like Society both aids and advances religious views.

However, Society is not sponsoring religion by helping victims of racial or religious discrimination. It is merely offering free legal assistance by commencing litigation in State X courts with an eye towards redressing the apparent instances of discrimination. The effect of these efforts is to advance equality in the Mayo community rather than to aid or advance religion.

Society is financially supported partially by a grant of funds from Agency. Agency administers a State X program providing funds to legal aid organizations. The funding appears to be a purely administrative function. There is no indication that Agency must actively supervise the activities of Society to ensure that the funds are being used for legal services. Further, Society is not totally funded by Agency. Church funds are also being used to fund Society's non-profit legal representation. Therefore, there appears to be no excessive government entanglement between the funds provided to Society by Agency.

The Taxpayers will be unsuccessful in their First Amendment Establishment Clause challenge and should be denied a judgment prohibiting Agency from granting funds to Society.

B. JAY v. CHURCH, SOCIETY AND AGENCY

Equal Protection

The Equal Protection Clause prohibits government regulations that discriminate on the basis of an arbitrary classification as individuals similarly situated must be treated the same.

Society is financially supported by Church and Agency. Agency's policy of providing public funds to legal aid organizations, such as Society, will be deemed a government regulation.

Moreover, Society is an arm of Agency who is charged with the responsibility of rendering free legal aid to Mayo citizens who have been victims of racial or religious discrimination. Society is composed exclusively of Church members who are licensed to practice in State X. Its apparent policy that its lawyers also be limited to members of Church is considered a government regulation.

Jay is a lawyer who has been admitted to practice in State X. He volunteered to join and work for Society without compensation but he was rejected because he is not a Church member. Society's membership policy discriminates on the basis of religion. Since employment in Society is decided upon Church affiliation rather than upon legal competency, an arbitrary classification exists. Jay is being treated differently than Church lawyers similarly situated who are permitted to work for Society solely on the basis of their Church membership.

Therefore, Jay has raised a proper Equal Protection Clause challenge.

State Action

In order to establish a violation of Equal Protection Clause, a nexus must be shown between the alleged discriminatory activity and the state's involvement.

Agency provides public funds to Society who assists Mayo citizens with their commencement of litigation arising from racial and religious discrimination. Since Agency administers the State X program that uses public funds in this manner, a significant state nexus can be shown between Agency's participation and Society's policy of using only Church lawyers to redress apparent instances of discrimination.

State action is present.

Classification Of The Discrimination

Laws which discriminate against a fundamental right are reviewed according to strict scrutiny. The government must show a compelling state interest and the least burdensome alternative available.

Jay will assert that exclusion of qualified lawyers from Society on the basis of non-Church affiliation is discrimination based on religion. Since freedom of religion is a fundamental right, the policy is subject to strict scrutiny. There is no compelling state interest to justify such a discriminatory policy requiring only Church members to serve victims of discrimination.

Society will counter that it requires its lawyers to be Church members in order to screen for qualified personnel. This facilitates the management of its program for providing free litigation assistance to Mayo citizens who have been victims of discrimination. Thus, it is a valid administrative decision.

Still, alternative measures exist that would accomplish the same objective with less harmful effects. If Society wishes to facilitate administration of its legal assistance program to ensure that only qualified lawyers participate, it can simply implement a qualifying test that all lawyers must pass in order to become a Society member. This would meet Society's objectives without eliminating competent licensed lawyers who would like to participate by rendering their legal expertise to those Mayo citizens who need free legal advise. Therefore, a least burdensome alternative is available.

Jay will be successful in proving that the defendants have engaged in discriminatory activities that violate the Fourteenth Amendment Equal Protection Clause.

C. STATE BAR v. SOCIETY

First Amendment - Freedom of Speech

First Amendment Freedom of Speech is a preferred right under the United States Constitution applicable to the states through the Fourteenth Amendment. It is not an absolute right and can be restricted by the government under certain situations.

The State X Bar Association is responsible for the enforcement of State X law regulating the practice of law. It has charged that the solicitation practices of Society's members violate the State X attorneys' professional disciplinary code prohibiting direct solicitation of clients and legal work by lawyers. Society's position is that the State Bar's challenge violates Society's First Amendment right to speech, a preferred right under the United States Constitution.
However, the State X Bar Association will contend that the right to free speech is not absolute. Because the Association has been charged with the power to regulate the practice of law in State X,

it has a substantial interest to justify its challenge.

Society will argue that it is a non-profit corporation. Its lawyers directly approach various Mayo citizens who appear to be victims of discrimination in order to assist them in redressing past wrongs that have been perpetrated against them. The Bar has the power to regulate solicitation only if the purpose of the solicitation is to promote profit-making for the Society lawyers. It must show evidence of objectionable practices actually occurring from the solicitation, or an actual or clearly threatened conflict of interest between lawyer and client created by the solicitation.

In this instance, Society lawyers are working free of charge on the behalf of discrimination victims. Many of these victims would not know they have legal rights if Society lawyers did not approach them to explain their rights. Without the free legal assistance that Society lawyers provide in commencing litigation to redress these instances of discrimination, the victims would be left without recourse.

In a case similar to the facts at hand, the United States Supreme Court ruled that when the NAACP encouraged, instructed, and offered to represent parents of black children to litigate against school segregation, such litigation was a form of political expression and political association; and since the NAACP sought no monetary gain, there was no danger of conflict of interest, which was the purpose of the state ban on solicitation of legal business (NAACP v. Button.)

Therefore, it appears that the State X Bar Association has violated Society's right to free speech guaranteed under the First Amendment. Thus, Bar will fail in its attempt to get an injunction.

Overbreadth

An overbroad law is one that regulates a substantial amount of constitutionally protected expression as well as expression that is not constitutionally protected.

The State X Bar Association has instituted an action in State X court seeking an injunction against Society and its members prohibiting any further solicitation activity by Society members. Although the Bar may regulate solicitation for the purpose of profit-making, it may not regulate solicitation where the purpose is to redress past instances of discrimination. Because the Bar is regulating both protected and unprotected expression, its regulation is overbroad.

Therefore, the regulation is void.

Vagueness

Where a statute provides no notice of what a reasonable person would have to do to conform his conduct to the terms of the statute, it will be deemed vague.

The State X Bar Association is seeking an injunction prohibiting any further solicitation activity by Society members. The meaning of "further solicitation activity" is subject to many interpretations. It could mean anything from directly approaching potential clients in order to promote business to casual conversation with those same persons who have questions about discriminatory practices and need free legal advise. There is a fine line between approaching victims of discrimination to explain their legal rights and soliciting clients.

Because the regulation contains imprecise language, State X's Bar Association has not provided sufficient notice to Society lawyers as to what "solicitation" actually means. In this instance, there is no way for a reasonable attorney to make that distinction and conform his conduct to the terms. To allow enforcement of this type of regulation would result in a "chilling effect" on Society's speech and association rights.

The regulation is void.

First Amendment - Freedom of Association

The First Amendment permits Freedom of Association without undue governmental restraint.

If the State X Bar Association regulation prohibiting "solicitation" were permitted, it would interfere with Society lawyers' freedom to associate with Mayo residents who appear to be victims of discrimination. If Society lawyers cannot directly contact these people without undue governmental restraint, it is unlikely that they could redress discrimination problems. The Bar Association cannot demonstrate a compelling state interest sufficient to justify interfering with the right of Mayo residents to associate with Society lawyers in order to receive free legal advise that ultimately benefits their interests.

The State X Bar Association has violated Society's First Amendment right to freedom of association.

SECTION VI

CRIMINAL PROCEDURE

CRIMINAL PROCEDURE

LEARN TO WRITE . . . THE RIGHT WAY®

CRIMINAL PROCEDURE QUESTION #1

STATE v. DAN

Fred, a federal customs inspector, saw Dan speak to Anon as Dan and Anon walked across the international border into the United States. Fred recognized Anon as a person who had been convicted of smuggling narcotics. Over Dan's protest, Fred searched luggage carried by Dan and Anon. Fred found a packet of glassine envelopes and some dextrose powder in Dan's suitcase and a large quantity of heroin in the lining of the suitcase carried by Anon.

Fred knew that dextrose powder is used to dilute heroin, and that heroin is sold in envelopes like those carried by Dan. Fred then ordered that Dan be searched in private by a physician who found a small quantity of heroin on Dan in a body cavity. Dan was thereupon arrested on a federal charge of importing narcotics without a permit.

Fred notified state narcotics agents of the arrest. Olson, a state agent, located Dan's car parked legally on a street in the United States near the border crossing. Olson impounded the car and, during a search of the car on the following day, discovered a large quantity of heroin. Dan was then charged with violation of a state statute prohibiting possession of narcotics for sale.

At a pre-trial bail hearing, Dan argued that he is entitled to have bail fixed, or, because he is indigent, to be released on his own recognizance. A state statute permits denial of pre-trial bail when a defendant poses too great a risk to society to remain free pending trial.

1. How should the federal court rule on Dan's motion to exclude the heroin found on his person from evidence at the federal trial? Discuss.

2. How should the state court rule on Dan's motion to exclude the heroin found in his car from evidence at the state trial? Discuss.

3. How should the state court rule on Dan's claim that he is entitled to have bail fixed or to be released pending trial on the state charge? Discuss.

IRAC OUTLINE SHEET

(I)	(R)	(A)	(C)

EXAMPLE OF PROPER IRAC OUTLINE

STATE v. DAN

1. MOTION TO EXCLUDE THE HEROIN FOUND ON DAN'S (D) PERSON?

(A) SEARCH OF D'S LUGGAGE

(I)	(R)	(A)	(C)
4TH AMENDMENT	Protects Against Unreasonable Search/Seizure	F a federal customs inspector Over D's protest F searched D's luggage without a warrant	Violation
	Governmental Intrusion	F a Federal customs inspector	
	Expectation Of Privacy	D's suitcase	
EXCEPTIONS TO WARRANTLESS SEARCH:			
BORDER SEARCH	Routine Searches	Searched luggage	Valid Exception
	Government Agent	F a custom inspector	
	International Border	F saw D speak to A as they walked across the int'l border into U.S.	
	No Warrant/Probable Cause Required	F recognized A as person who had been convicted of smuggling narcotics F searched luggage (reasonable suspicion drugs?) (public policy-relaxed standards)	

(B) SEARCH OF D'S PERSON

(I)	(R)	(A)	(C)
4TH AMENDMENT	Protects Against Unreasonable Search/Seizure	F ordered that D to be searched in private by a physician without a warrant	Violation
	Governmental Intrusion	Customs inspector/in private by a physician	
	Expectation Of Privacy	Body cavity	
EXCEPTIONS TO WARRANTLESS SEARCH:			
BORDER SEARCH	Routine Searches	Int'l border Luggage searched supra/found packet of glassine envelopes & some dextrose powder in D's suitcase D's person searched (reasonable?)	Valid Exception
	Government Agent	Supra	
	International Border	Supra	
	No Warrant/Probable Cause Required	Fred knew dextrose powder used to dilute heroin & that heroin is sold in envelopes like those carried by D Large quantity of heroin in lining of suitcase carried by A	
DUE PROCESS BODY SEARCH	Search Must Be Reasonable	F ordered D searched in private by physician who found a small quantity of heroin on D in a body cavity	Evidence Admissible Motion Denied

2. MOTION TO EXCLUDE THE HEROIN FOUND IN DAN'S (D) CAR?

(I)	(R)	(A)	(C)
4TH AMENDMENT	Protects Against Unreasonable Search/Seizure	O located D's car parked legally on a street in the U.S. near border crossing O impounded D's car/searched following day without a warrant	Violation
	Governmental Intrusion	O, a state narcotics agent	
	Expectation Of Privacy	D's car parked legally	

(I)	(R)	(A)	(C)
EXCEPTIONS TO WARRANTLESS SEARCH:			
IMPOUNDMENT/INVENTORY SEARCH	Auto	Car legally parked in U.S. near border	Invalid Exception
	Lawful Impoundment	O impounded the car?	
	Inventory To Protect Defendants Possessions & Police From Theft Allegations	Searched car on the following day Discovered a large quantity of heroin	
AUTOMOBILE EXCEPTION	Mobility	D arrested/car parked legally	Invalid Exception
	Probable Cause	No facts	
PUBLIC SAFETY	Search Of Auto	Car searched without warrant	Invalid Exception
	Public Safety Threatened	D arrested/car parked legally	
STANDING	Common Law: Proprietary/Possessory Right	D's car parked legally on street supra	Standing
	Modern Law: Reasonable Expectation Of Privacy Totality Of Circumstances	D's car supra	
EXCLUSIONARY RULE	Evidence Of Illegal Search Inadmissible Fruit Of Poisonous Tree	Search of car No warrant Heroin	Evidence Excluded

3. DAN'S (D) CLAIM TO HAVE BAIL FIXED OR HE BE RELEASED PENDING TRIAL?

(I)	(R)	(A)	(C)
8TH AMENDMENT	8 TH Amendment Prohibits Excessive Bail	At pre-trial hearing, D argued that he is entitled to have bail fixed A state statute permits denial of pre-trial bail when a defendant poses too great a risk to society to remain free pending trial D arrested supra	No Violation
	8 TH Amendment Not Binding On States	State statute	
PURPOSE OF BAIL	Assure Presence At Trial	D charged with violation of state statute prohibiting possession of narcotics for sale	No Violation
	Danger To Society	D charged with drug smuggling	
RIGHTS OF INDIGENTS TO BAIL	Setting Bail Discretionary With Court	D argued he's indigent & entitled to be released on own recognizance (due process satisfied indigents given no greater rights)	No Protection Afforded

EXAMPLE OF IRAC CRIMINAL PROCEDURE ISSUE

(I) **Fourth Amendment**

(R) The Fourth Amendment, applicable to the state through the Fourteenth Amendment, protects against (1) unreasonable searches and seizures by a (2) governmental intrusion upon a (3) reasonable expectation of privacy.

(A) Fred is a federal customs inspector. Over Dan's protest, he searched Dan's luggage without a warrant. Fred's failure to obtain a warrant prior to the search indicates that he conducted (1) an unreasonable search.

Fred conducted the search in his capacity as a federal customs inspector. His actions as an inspector will constitute a (2) governmental intrusion.

The suitcase canted by Dan was the object of the search. One normally has a (3) reasonable expectation of privacy in his luggage and the contents therein.

(C) Therefore, the search of the luggage falls within the fourth amendment. Since it was conducted without a warrant, it is presumed invalid unless the state can show an applicable exception.

SUGGESTED MODEL ANSWER

1. MOTION TO EXCLUDE HEROIN FOUND ON DAN'S PERSON?

(A) SEARCH OF DAN'S LUGGAGE

Fourth Amendment

The Fourth Amendment, applicable to the states through the Fourteenth Amendment, protects against unreasonable searches and seizures by a governmental intrusion upon a reasonable expectation of privacy.

Fred is a federal customs inspector. Over Dan's protest, he searched Dan's luggage without a warrant. Fred's failure to obtain a warrant prior to the search indicates that he conducted an unreasonable search.

Fred conducted the search in his capacity as a federal customs inspector. His actions as an inspector will constitute a governmental intrusion.

The suitcase carried by Dan was the object of the search. One normally has a reasonable expectation of privacy in his luggage and the contents therein.

Therefore, the search of the luggage falls within the Fourth Amendment. Since it was conducted without a warrant, it is presumed invalid unless the state can show an applicable exception.

Exception To Warrantless Search

Border Search

Routine searches by government agents at an international border or its functional equivalent may be conducted without a warrant or probable cause.

When Dan walked across the international border into the United States, a routine search of his luggage was conducted by Fred, a government agent. Fred's actions were motivated by his recognition of Anon who had been previously convicted of smuggling narcotics and who was speaking to Dan as they walked across the border. These facts and circumstances may have been enough to give Fred a bona fide reasonable suspicion and sufficient belief that Dan was smuggling narcotics.

The public policy concept of protection of the national sovereignty from the possibility that drugs are being smuggled across an international border have resulted in relaxed standards that would permit the search. Therefore, Fred did not need a warrant or probable cause to conduct the search of the luggage.

The border search will be a valid exception to the Fourth Amendment.

(B) SEARCH OF DAN'S PERSON

Fourth Amendment

Defined supra.

Fred ordered that Dan be searched in private by a physician. Since he did so without a warrant, an unreasonable search took place.

The physician carried out the search at the direction of the federal customs inspector constituting a governmental intrusion. The physician examined Dan's body and searched his body cavities where he had a reasonable expectation of privacy.

Therefore, the search falls within the Fourth Amendment protection. Since the search was conducted without a warrant, it is presumed invalid unless the state can show an applicable exception.

Border Search

Defined supra.

When Dan's luggage was routinely searched at the international border, Fred found a packet of glassine envelopes, the type used to package and sell heroin. Fred knew that this item could be combined with the dextrose powder to dilute heroin. Since both were in Dan's suitcase, the discovery gave rise to the routine search of Dan's person. Such evidence, in conjunction with the large quantity of heroin found in Anon's suitcase, supports Fred's reasonable suspicion as a federal customs inspector that Dan might be attempting to smuggle illegal narcotics in his body cavities across the international border.

In order to protect the national sovereignty of the United States from illegal heroin importation, public policy will allow the search even in the absence of a warrant or probable cause.

The border search will be a valid exception to the Fourth Amendment.

Due Process - Body Search

When a body search is conducted, it must be done in a reasonable manner in accordance with due process standards.

Fred ordered Dan to be searched in private by a physician who was ostensibly qualified to do so. The physician found a small quantity of heroin in Dan's body cavity. The body search appears to have been done in a reasonable manner in accordance with due process standards.

Therefore, the heroin found on Dan's person is admissible. The federal court should deny Dan's motion to exclude the heroin.

2. MOTION TO EXCLUDE THE HEROIN FOUND IN DAN'S CAR?

Fourth Amendment

Defined supra.

Olson located Dan's car parked legally on a street in the United States near the border crossing. It was impounded and searched without a warrant. Olson's failure to obtain a warrant prior to the search indicates that he conducted an unreasonable search and seizure. The search was conducted by Olsen, a state narcotics agent. Since he was acting in his law enforcement capacity, his actions would suffice as a governmental intrusion. Dan's car was the object of the search. One normally has a reasonable expectation of privacy in his car and the contents contained therein.

Therefore, the search of the car falls within the Fourth Amendment. Since it was conducted without a warrant, it is presumed invalid unless the state can show an applicable exception.

Exceptions To Warrantless Search

Impoundment/Inventory Search

The police may search a automobile which is lawfully impounded to protect the defendant's possessions and to protect the police from theft allegations provided there are standard operating procedures so allowing.

Olsen, a state narcotics agent, was notified that Dan had been arrested on a federal charge of importing narcotics. Thus, when he located Dan's car, he recognized the potential that drug related evidence could be in the automobile. Although Dan's car was legally parked, it had been left unattended on a city street near an international border where it could be stolen. This justifies Olsen's decision to impound the car. The subsequent search was intended to protect Dan's possessions while he was in custody and to protect the police from theft allegations.

However, the facts indicate that the car was legally parked. Absent facts showing that the police had reasonable belief that the car contained contraband, no justification exists to support an immediate impoundment of the car without a warrant.

Further, the car was not searched until the following day. The facts do not indicate that standard operating procedures permitted the search. It is unlikely that the police were solely motivated by a desire to protect the defendant's possessions or themselves from theft allegations. If they had been, they would have impounded and inventoried the car on the same day that they arrested Dan. Therefore, the impoundment is unlawful and the subsequent search is invalid.

The impoundment/inventory exception will not be a valid exception to the Fourth Amendment.

Automobile Exception

The courts have decided that the mobility of cars may justify an immediate search of the entire automobile provided there is probable cause to believe that contraband is in the car.

The State will contend that Dan had been arrested. His car was left on the street. When a car is left unattended on a city street near an international border, a high potential exists for vandalism and theft. The danger created by the car's potential for mobility justifies Olsen's act of impounding the car and then conducting the search.

Yet, there are no facts to indicate that Olsen could not have posted surveillance around the car to prevent any threat of mobility while he obtained a valid search warrant. Moreover, and most importantly, there are no facts providing probable cause to search.

Therefore, the automobile exception will not provide a valid exception to the Fourth Amendment.

Public Safety

The police may conduct a warrantless search of an automobile if the public safety is threatened.

Dan's car was parked near the border. Dan had been arrested and his car had been left unattended and could have easily been stolen. Since it could have contained illegal drugs, a warrantless search of the automobile is justified as the public safety could be threatened.

However, there are no facts to indicate that the car created an immediate threat to the public safety even if it did contain heroin. The possibility for theft is speculative at best. Olsen had plenty of time to obtain a warrant before he impounded the car and later searched it.

The public safety exception will not be a valid exception to the Fourth Amendment.

Standing To Invoke The Exclusionary Rule

At common law, the party seeking to exclude evidence must have a proprietary or possessory right in the evidence seized. Modernly, the court will examine the claimant's reasonable expectation of privacy under the totality of the circumstances.

Dan owned the car, the object of the search. He retained both a proprietary and possessory interest in it while it was legally parked on the street. Based on the same facts, he would have a reasonable expectation of privacy in its integrity and the contents contained therein, under the totality of circumstances test.

Therefore, under both the common law and the modern law, Dan has standing to assert the exclusionary rule.

Exclusionary Rule

Pursuant to the Wong Sun case, evidence of an illegal search is inadmissible as a fruit of the poisonous tree.

The heroin evidence was found in Dan's car as the result of the illegal warrantless search. Therefore, it should be inadmissible as a fruit of the poisonous tree.

In this case, the exclusionary rule applies. The court should grant Dan's motion to exclude the heroin found in his car and rule that the evidence is inadmissible.

3. DAN'S CLAIM THAT HE IS ENTITLED TO HAVE BAIL FIXED OR TO BE RELEASED PENDING TRIAL?

Eighth Amendment

The Eighth Amendment guarantees that excessive bail shall not be required. It is not binding on the states through the Fourteenth Amendment.

Dan will assert that the state statute permitting denial of his pre-trial bail violates his Eighth Amendment right. He has the right to have bail fixed in an amount not considered excessive so that he can be released on his own recognizance in order to assist in the preparation of his own defense.

Nevertheless, the Eighth Amendment is not binding on the states through the Fourteenth Amendment. As such, the state may set its own standard for bail. It may deny bail when it has grounds to believe a defendant poses too great a risk to society to remain free on bail pending trial.

The state statute will not violate the Eighth Amendment.

Purpose Of Bail

Bail is intended to assure a defendant's presence at time of trial. It may be denied to those who pose a danger to society before the time of trial.

Dan had been arrested and charged with possession of narcotics for sale following a search where narcotics were discovered in his luggage and body cavities. He was known to have crossed an international border. The sale of heroin is known to generate great sums of money. Thus, no amount of bail could be reasonably calculated to assure Dan's presence at time of trial.

Moreover, these facts create a sufficient justification for the court to infer that Dan's release would create a potential danger to society if he were to flee the country or continue with his alleged drug smuggling.

These circumstances would reasonably outweigh any rights that Dan could raise in support of bail or release on his own recognizance.

Dan's Eighth Amendment rights have not been violated.

Rights Of Indigents To Bail

Setting bail is considered a matter within the discretion of the trial court.

Dan argues that he is indigent. He will contend that the money bail system is unfair to indigents since those with money are released while the poor have to remain in jail.

As such, he should be afforded a greater protection because he is indigent. He should be released from custody on his own recognizance until the time of trial.

However, states are not bound to afford indigents any greater right to bail than it does to non-indigents. Because Dan creates a risk to society, denial of bail and refusal to release Dan on his own recognizance is a valid exercise of the court's discretion.

Dan is not entitled to any greater rights as an indigent under the Eighth Amendment.

CRIMINAL PROCEDURE QUESTION #2

STATE v. BOB

Acting with probable cause, but without a warrant, police forcibly entered Bob's mobile home, a licensed motorized vehicle which was parked in a motor park and connected to utilities. They seized a quantity of cocaine found in the mobile home. Although Bob lived in the mobile home, he was not present at the time the police entered. Bob has been charged with violating Section 52 of the State X Criminal Code which makes it a felony to: "knowingly possess cocaine."

Bob made a timely pretrial motion to suppress the cocaine under the Fourth Amendment. The court denied the motion.

Bob, who is indigent, made a timely pretrial motion for leave to represent himself at trial and for court appointed "stand-by" counsel who would be available to assist if Bob desired help. The court denied Bob's motion for standby counsel. The court advised Bob that he could either proceed pro se, or have counsel appointed to conduct the entire defense. Bob competently waived the appointment of counsel. He then defended himself at trial.

At trial the cocaine was admitted in evidence over Bob's renewed objection. Bob testified that he did not realize the substance was cocaine and that he had believed it was a legally possessable cocaine-like substance which he intended to give to his friends as a joke.

The court instructed the jury: "If you find beyond a reasonable doubt that the defendant possessed cocaine, you should find him guilty unless you also find that he has proved by a preponderance of the evidence that he reasonably mistook the cocaine for a legally possessable substance."

Did the court err in:

1. Admitting the cocaine as evidence? Discuss.

2. Denying stand-by counsel? Discuss.

3. Giving the above jury instruction? Discuss.

IRAC OUTLINE SHEET

(I)	(R)	(A)	(C)

EXAMPLE OF PROPER IRAC OUTLINE

DID THE COURT ERR IN:

(1) ADMITTING THE COCAINE AS EVIDENCE?

(I)	(R)	(A)	(C)
4TH AMENDMENT	Protects Against Unreasonable Search/Seizure	Acting with probable cause but without a warrant police forcibly entered B's mobile home	Violation
	Governmental Intrusion	State X police	
	Expectation Of Privacy	Mobile home, a licensed motorized vehicle which was parked in a motor park & connected to utilities Although B lived there, he was not present at the home the police entered	
EXCEPTIONS TO WARRANTLESS SEARCH:			
AUTOMOBILE	Probable Cause	Acting with probable cause but without a warrant Quantity of cocaine found in mobile home	Arguable Exception
	Mobile Home	Mobile home, licensed motorized vehicle, parked in a motor park	
	Mobility/Use	Connected to utilities supra Bob lived in mobile home	
EXIGENT CIRCUMSTANCES	Hot Pursuit Of Suspect	Mobile home supra B lived there but not present supra	Arguable Exception
	Loss/Destruction Of Evidence	Cocaine found supra B was not present supra	
STANDING	Common Law: Proprietary/Possessory Right	B lived there but was not present supra	Standing
	Modern Law: Reasonable Expectation Of Privacy Totality Of Circumstances	B lived there but was not present supra	
EXCLUSIONARY RULE	Evidence Of Illegal Search Inadmissible	Police searched & seized a quantity of cocaine found in the mobile home	Arguable
	Fruit Of Poisonous Tree	Without a warrant supra B made a timely motion to suppress the cocaine	
2. DENYING STAND-BY COUNSEL?			
6th AMENDMENT RIGHT TO COUNSEL	All Felony Prosecutions	B has been charged with violating section 52 of State X criminal code which makes it a felony to "knowingly possess cocaine"	Right To Counsel
	Other Prosecutions	No facts	
	Actual Loss Liberty	B has been charged B defended himself at trial	
	Actual Imprisonment	Conviction?	
6Th AMENDMENT INDIGENT'S RIGHT TO COUNSEL	Appointed Counsel	B made a timely pre-trial motion for leave to represent himself & court appointed stand-by counsel to assist if B desired help	No Court Err

(I)	(R)	(A)	(C)
	Indigents	B is indigent	
	Trial	At trial	
	Stand-By Counsel	B made a motion for stand-by counsel who would be available to assist if B desired help Court denied B's motion	
<u>WAIVER OF COUNSEL</u>	Knowingly	B made a timely pretrial motion for leave to represent himself at trial supra The court advised B that he could either proceed pro se or have counsel appointed to conduct the entire defense	No Court Err
	Intelligently	B waived the appointment of counsel	
	Voluntarily	He then defended himself at trial	
<u>COMPETENCY</u>	Court Determines	B made a motion to represent himself The court advised supra	No Court Err
	Ability To Waive	B competently waived supra	

3. <u>GIVING THE JURY INSTRUCTION</u>?

(I)	(R)	(A)	(C)
<u>BURDEN OF PERSUASION</u>	State Burden Of Proof	B charged with State X code which makes it a felony to "knowingly possess cocaine	Court Erred
	Elements Of Offense	B testified that he did not realize the substance was cocaine B believed it was a legally possessable cocaine like substance which he intended to give to his friends as a joke	
	Beyond A Reasonable Doubt	The court instructed: If you find beyond a reasonable doubt the defendant possessed cocaine, you should find him guilty unless you also find that he has proved by a preponderance of the evidence that he reasonably mistook the cocaine for a legally possessable substance	

EXAMPLE OF IRAC CRIMINAL PROCEDURE ISSUE

(I) **Exigent Circumstances**

(R) A warrantless search may be conducted when (1) officers are in hot pursuit of a suspect or (2) when the delay caused by obtaining a warrant would permit evidence to be lost or destroyed.

(A) The State will assert that the motorized nature of Bob's mobile home created the opportunity for Bob to escape from State X. In order to prevent Bob from using the mobile home to flee the jurisdiction, the warrantless search was reasonably necessary.

However, although Bob lived there, he was not present at the time of the search. There is no indication that he would have had the opportunity to resist or flee before the police had time to obtain a warrant. Since there is no indication that the police were in (1) hot pursuit of Bob when they conducted the search, the warrantless search cannot be justified on this basis.

The facts indicate that a large quantity of cocaine was found inside Bob's mobile home. The police had probable cause to believe that the contraband would be seized if the search was conducted without delay. There was no indication how long Bob had been gone or when he would return. Since he lived there, he could come home at any time and drive away from the motor park taking the contraband with him. Due to the (2) potential loss or destruction of the evidence, the police had little choice but to conduct the search without a warrant.

(C) Exigent circumstances will arguably be a valid exception to the fourth amendment. The court did not err by denying Bob's pretrial motion to suppress the cocaine.

SUGGESTED MODEL ANSWER

STATE v. BOB

DID THE COURT ERR IN:

1. ADMITTING THE COCAINE AS EVIDENCE?

Fourth Amendment

The Fourth Amendment, applicable to the states through the Fourteenth Amendment, protects against unreasonable searches and seizures by a governmental intrusion upon a reasonable expectation of privacy.

Although the police acted with probable cause when they forcibly entered Bob's mobile home, they did so without a warrant. Their failure to obtain a warrant prior to entry indicates that they conducted an unreasonable search and seizure.

The search of Bob's mobile home was conducted by State X police acting in their law enforcement capacity. This conduct is sufficient to show a governmental intrusion.

The mobile home was licensed and parked in a motor park where it was connected to utilities. Although Bob lived there, he was not home at the time the police entered. Nevertheless, he had a reasonable expectation of privacy in the integrity of his mobile home and the contents contained therein.

Therefore, the search and seizure of the cocaine falls within the Fourth Amendment. Since it was conducted without a warrant, it is presumed invalid unless the State can show an applicable exception.

Exceptions To A Warrantless Search

Automobile Exception

Probable cause may justify a warrantless search of a mobile home subject to mobility and use factors.

The State will contend that it had the right to search Bob's mobile home without a warrant because probable cause existed to suspect that his motorized vehicle contained evidence of a crime or contraband. In this case, the police had a reasonable suspicion and articulable facts to believe the mobile home contained contraband. They acted pursuant to that belief by searching it. The search resulted in the seizure of a quantity of cocaine.

Bob will counter that the mobile home was parked in a motor park and was connected to utilities at the time of the search. The fact that it was hooked up to utilities indicates that the mobile home was not capable of being used as a motorized vehicle at the time of the search. Further, Bob lived there and used the mobile home as his place of residence rather than for a means of transportation. Therefore, due to mobility and use factors, the warrantless entry by the police was unjustified.

However, a mobile home that is a licensed motorized vehicle generally possesses the same attributes of mobility as an automobile. Connecting or unconnecting a mobile home to or from utilities in a motor park is usually a simple and quick procedure. As long as a mobile home maintains the motorized equipment that gives it the capability of mobility, it can be driven away very easily. The Supreme Court has held that citizens have a lesser expectation of privacy in mobile vehicles than they would in a permanent house. Therefore, the police acted justifiably when they searched Bob's mobile home.

The automobile exception will arguably be a valid exception to the Fourth Amendment. The court did not err by denying Bob's pretrial motion to suppress the cocaine.

Exigent Circumstances

A warrantless search may be conducted when officers are in hot pursuit of a suspect or when the delay caused by obtaining a warrant would permit evidence to be lost or destroyed.

The State will assert that the motorized nature of Bob's mobile home created the opportunity for Bob to escape from State X. In order to prevent Bob from using the mobile home to flee the jurisdiction, the warrantless search was reasonably necessary.

However, although Bob lived there, he was not present at the time of the search. There is no indication that he would have had the opportunity to resist or flee before the police had time to obtain a warrant. Since there is no indication that the police were in hot pursuit of Bob when they conducted the search, the warrantless search cannot be justified on this basis.

The facts indicate that a large quantity of cocaine was found inside Bob's mobile home. The police had probable cause to believe that the contraband would be seized if the search was conducted without delay. There was no indication how long Bob had been gone or when he would return. Since he lived there, he could come home at any time and drive away from the motor park taking the contraband with him. Due to the potential loss or destruction of the evidence, the police had little choice but to conduct the search without a warrant.

Exigent circumstances will arguably be a valid exception to the Fourth Amendment. The court did not err by denying Bob's pretrial motion to suppress the cocaine.

Standing To Invoke The Exclusionary Rule

At common law, the party seeking to exclude evidence must have a proprietary or possessory right in the evidence seized. Modernly, the court will examine the claimant's reasonable expectation of privacy under the totality of the circumstances.

If the State is unsuccessful in proving a valid exception to the Fourth Amendment, Bob will argue that he lived in the mobile home where the cocaine was seized. Because the facts indicate that it was Bob's mobile home, it appears that he had both a proprietary and a possessory right in the mobile home and the contents contained therein. Further, there is no doubt that Bob would have a reasonable expectation of privacy in his mobile home under the totality of circumstances test.

Therefore, both under the common law and the modern law, Bob has standing to assert the exclusionary rule.

Exclusionary Rule

Pursuant to the Wong Sun case, evidence of an illegal search is inadmissible as a fruit of the poisonous tree.

If the cocaine evidence was seized as the result of an alleged illegal warrantless search of Bob's mobile home, it should be inadmissible as a fruit of the poisonous tree.

Therefore, the court may have erred by admitting the evidence and should have granted Bob's motion to exclude the cocaine.

2. DENYING STAND-BY COUNSEL?

Sixth Amendment - The Right To Counsel

The Sixth Amendment right to counsel, applicable to the states through the Fourteenth Amendment, requires that counsel be available in all felony prosecutions plus any other prosecution as to which there is an actual loss of liberty, i.e., as to which actual imprisonment is imposed.

Bob has been charged with violating Section 52 of the State X Criminal Code which makes it a felony to "knowingly possess cocaine." He is being prosecuted for this felony. Because he has been charged and is defending himself at trial, it can be inferred that he has sustained an actual loss of liberty during the proceeding. If Bob is convicted of the felony, actual imprisonment is sure to result.

Bob is entitled to counsel under the Sixth Amendment.

Sixth Amendment - Indigent's Right To Appointed Counsel

The Sixth Amendment guarantees that the state provide appointed counsel to indigents at time of trial. However, there is no guaranteed right to stand-by counsel. Most courts will allow the defendant to either represent himself or have a lawyer represent him at trial. They do not allow the defendant to handle parts of the case while a lawyer handles other parts.

Bob's timely pre-trial motion was for leave to represent himself at trial and for court appointed "stand-by" counsel who would be available to assist if Bob desired help. The Sixth Amendment guarantees that State X provide appointed counsel to Bob because he is indigent. Since he is being prosecuted for violating a State X Criminal Code, it appears Bob is preparing to go to trial on that charge and apparently could not afford to retain his own private counsel. However, there is no guaranteed right to "stand-by" counsel. The court may allow Bob to represent himself but it may not allow Bob to handle some aspects of his case while, at the same time, having counsel available at the state's expense to help Bob with other aspects of the case as Bob desires.

The court did not err when it denied Bob's motion for stand-by counsel.

Right To Waive Counsel

A defendant may waive his Sixth Amendment right to counsel if he does so knowingly, intelligently, and voluntarily.

Bob made a timely pretrial motion for leave to represent himself at trial. The court advised Bob that he could either proceed pro se or have counsel appointed to conduct the entire defense. Bob was effectively advised of his right to counsel and the consequence of proceeding pro se. Thus, Bob was knowingly aware of his rights. He elected to waive counsel and exercise his right to represent himself at trial. Since the waiver was made after advise from the court, it appears that Bob exercised his rights intelligently and voluntarily.

Bob has validly waived his right to counsel. His Sixth Amendment rights have not been violated. The court did not err.

Competency

The court determines the defendant's ability to waive his rights.

As previously discussed, Bob made a timely motion for leave to represent himself at trial and for "stand-by" counsel who would be available to assist him at trial. The court advised Bob that he could either proceed pro se or have counsel appointed to conduct the entire defense. Bob competently waived the appointment of counsel. It appears that Bob had the ability to defend himself at trial and, on this basis, the court determined that he had the right of self-representation. Since the court advised Bob of his right to counsel and he competently waived the right, the court properly exercised its discretion by allowing Bob to proceed.

The court did not err.

3. GIVING THE JURY INSTRUCTION?

Burden Of Persuasion

When prosecuting an accused, the state has the burden of proving each and every element of the charged offense beyond a reasonable doubt.

Bob was charged with a State X criminal code which makes it a felony to "knowingly possess cocaine." It is incumbent upon the state prosecutor to carry its burden of proof as to the elements of the offense.

Bob testified that he did not realize the substance was cocaine. Instead, he believed that it was a legally possessable cocaine-like substance that he intended to give to his friends as a joke. This testimony directly impacted on the State's ability to prove the element of intent to "knowingly" possess. If the jury chose to believe Bob's testimony, the State would not be able to prove the "knowingly" element of the offense.

When the court instructed the jury "If you find beyond a reasonable doubt that the defendant possessed cocaine, you should find him guilty unless you also find that he has proved by a preponderance of the evidence that he reasonably mistook the cocaine for a legally possessable substance," it improperly shifted the burden of persuasion from the state prosecutor to the defendant.

Further, the court failed to include that element of "knowingly" in its instructions of the law. Bob admitted that he possessed the cocaine. However, he testified that he didn't know that it was cocaine. It is not Bob's burden to prove by a preponderance of evidence that he reasonably mistook the substance for a legally possessable substance. It is the State's burden to prove beyond a reasonable doubt that Bob knowingly possessed the cocaine.

The court erred by giving the above jury instruction. It has abused its discretion by improperly shifting the burden of persuasion to the defendant.

CRIMINAL PROCEDURE QUESTION #3

STATE v. DEFT

Deft was formally charged with a criminal offense punishable with a ninety-day maximum jail term and/or a $500 fine. As Deft was being brought by a policeman to the courtroom for arraignment, Witt, who had witnessed the charged offense and was asked by the prosecutor to be present at Deft's arraignment, said to the policeman, "Yes, that's the guy!"

At the arraignment, Deft established his indigency and requested appointment of counsel and trial by jury. The arraignment judge denied both requests without explanation.

Representing himself in the trial court, Deft moved to exclude evidence of Witt's statement to the policeman that he recognized Deft at the arraignment, and to prevent identification of Deft by Witt at trial. The trial judge agreed to exclude evidence of Witt's statement to the policeman but refused to prevent any potential identification of Deft by Witt at trial.

After the foregoing rulings, Deft negotiated a plea bargain with the prosecutor under which Deft agreed to enter a plea of guilty without admitting that he was, in fact, guilty, and the State agreed that it would not request a jail term. The plea agreement was explained to the court. The judge then advised Deft of the constitutional rights he would waive by pleading guilty and also told Deft the maximum statutory penalty that could be imposed. The judge explained that the plea agreement did not limit the court's discretion in imposing sentence. Deft then waived his rights and agreed to go forward with the plea. After the prosecutor made a proffer of evidence to establish a factual basis for the charge, the judge accepted Deft's plea of guilty, even though Deft told the judge he was really innocent. Deft was sentenced to a fine of $500 and thirty-day suspended jail term.

Deft has appealed. The jurisdiction permits an appeal following a plea of guilty. You may assume that each issue raised by Deft is a proper subject for appeal notwithstanding the guilty plea.

Deft argues in the appellate court that his conviction must be reversed on federal constitutional grounds because:

1. He was denied his right to appointed counsel.
2. He was denied his right to trial by jury.
3. Any identification of Deft by Witt was inadmissible at trial.
4. His plea was not shown to be voluntary and intelligent and should not have been accepted since he had maintained that he was innocent.

How should the appellate court rule on each of Deft's arguments? Discuss.

IRAC OUTLINE SHEET

(I)	(R)	(A)	(C)

EXAMPLE OF PROPER IRAC OUTLINE

HOW SHOULD THE APPELLATE COURT RULE ON EACH OF DEFT'S ARGUMENTS?

1. DENIAL OF RIGHT TO APPOINTED COUNSEL

(I)	(R)	(A)	(C)
6TH AMENDMENT	All Felony Prosecutions	D formally charged with a criminal offense Other prosecutions punishable with a 90 day maximum jail term and/or a $500 fine At arraignment, D established indigence & requested appointed counsel Requests denied without explanation	Violation
	Actual Loss Liberty	As D was being brought by a policeman to the courtroom for arraignment	
	Actual Imprisonment	D negotiated a plea bargain with the prosecutor under which D agreed to enter a plea of guilty without admitting that he was in fact guilty & that the state would not request a jail term. Plea explained to the court The judge advised D of the constitutional rights he would waive/told D that maximum penalty could be imposed The judge explained that the plea arrangement did not limit court's discretion in imposing sentence D then waived rights & agreed to go forward with plea	
	Suspended Sentence	The judge accepted the plea & sentenced D to a fine of $500 & a 30 day suspended jail term	

2. DENIAL OF RIGHT TO TRIAL BY JURY

(I)	(R)	(A)	(C)
6TH AMENDMENT	Serious Offense	D was formally charged with a criminal offense D requested trial by jury	No Violation
	Potential Sentence Over Six Months	Offense punishable with a 90 day maximum jail term and/or a $500 fine Request denied without explanation	

3. ANY IDENTIFICATION INADMISSIBLE AT TRIAL

(I)	(R)	(A)	(C)
6TH AMENDMENT ARRAIGNMENT IDENTIFICATION	Lineup/Face-Face Confrontation	As D was being brought by a policeman to the court room for arraignment, W, who witnessed the charged offense & was asked by the prosecutor to be present at D's arraignment, said to the policeman "yes, that's the guy"	Violation
	After Formal Charges	D was formally charged	
	Critical Stage	At the arraignment, D requested appointment of counsel	
DUE PROCESS	Identification Procedure	D's arraignment supra W asked to be present supra	Proper Ruling
	Unreliable	No other suspects present The trial judge agreed to exclude evidence of W's statement to the policeman	
5TH AMENDMENT COURT TRIAL IDENTIFICATION	In Court Identification	Representing himself at trial, D moved to prevent identification of D by W at trial	No Violation
	Self Incrimination	The court refused to prevent any potential ID of D by W at trial	

(I)	(R)	(A)	(C)
6TH AMENDMENT COURT TRIAL IDENTIFICATION	Independent Of The Pre-Trial Identification	W witnessed the charge offense supra Representing himself at trial, D moved to prevent identification of D by W at trial The court refused to prevent any potential ID by W at trial	No Violation
4. INEFFECTIVE GUILTY PLEA			
6TH AMENDMENT RIGHT TO A FAIR TRIAL	Fair/Impartial Trial	D negotiated a plea bargain The judge advised D of the constitutional rights he would waive by pleading guilty D then waived his rights & agreed to go forward with the plea D told the judge he was really innocent	No Violation
ACCEPTANCE OF A GUILTY PLEA	Open Court Record	The judge then advised D supra Told D of maximum statutory penalty	No Violation
	Voluntary	D negotiated a plea bargain with the prosecutor under which D agreed to enter a plea of guilty without admitting that he was in fact guilty & the state agreed that it would not request a jail term	
	Intelligent	Judge told D the maximum penalty supra Judge explained that the plea agreement did not limit the court's discretion in imposing sentence (understand consequences?) D then waived his rights supra After the prosecutor made a proffer of evidence to establish a factual bass for the charge, the judge accepted D's plea of guilty even though D told the judge he was really innocent	

EXAMPLE OF IRAC CRIMINAL PROCEDURE ISSUE

(I) **Acceptance of A Guilty Plea**

(R) When accepting an accused's plea of guilty, the court must address the defendant personally in (1) open court on the record to determine that the plea is (2) voluntary and (3) intelligent.

(A) After Deft negotiated his plea bargain with the prosecutor under which he agreed to enter a plea of guilty without admitting that he was, in fact guilty, and the State agreed that it would not request jail time, the plea was explained to the court. The judge then advised Deft of the constitutional rights he would waive by pleading guilty. He also told Deft of the maximum statutory penalty that could be imposed. Deft waived his rights and agreed to go forward with his plea. By its instruction to Deft in (1) open court and on the record, the court advised Deft of the nature of the charge, the maximum penalty possible, the fact that he had the right to plead not guilty and the fact that by pleading guilty, he waived his right to a jury trial. The Court's explanation was sufficient to ensure that Deft knew of and understood the charges. Therefore, Deft's decision to enter his plea was (2) voluntary.

Further, the judge told Deft of the maximum statutory penalty that could be imposed explaining that the plea did not limit the court's discretion in imposing the maximum statutory penalty. Despite Deft's prior agreement with the prosecution, he understood the consequences of entering a guilty plea even though he maintained that he was innocent. The instruction given by the judge was sufficient to give Deft a reasonable basis upon which to understand the consequences of the plea bargain. By waiving his rights, authorizing the prosecutor to make a proffer of evidence to establish a factual basis for the charge and then entering his plea, Deft exercised his right to make (3) an intelligent decision concerning his guilty plea.

(C) The Court properly accepted Deft's guilty plea. The appellate court should rule that his conviction should not be reversed.

SUGGESTED MODEL ANSWER

STATE v. DEFT

HOW SHOULD THE APPELLATE COURT RULE ON EACH OF DEFT'S ARGUMENTS?

1. Denial of Right To Appointed Counsel

Sixth Amendment

The Sixth Amendment right to counsel, applicable to the states through the Fourteenth Amendment, requires that counsel be available in all felony prosecutions plus any other prosecution as to which there is an actual loss of liberty, i.e., as to which actual imprisonment is imposed. If an indigent defendant receives a suspended sentence, counsel must be provided.

Deft was formally charged with a criminal offense punishable with a 90 day maximum jail term and/or a $500 fine. At the arraignment, Deft established indigence and requested appointed counsel. His request was denied without explanation.

The sentence for the charged offense was a 90 day maximum jail term and/or a $500 fine. Based on the maximum sentence that could be imposed, it appears that Deft's alleged crime does not satisfy the requirement that a felony prosecution be involved in order for the court to appoint counsel.

However, any prosecution will suffice. Deft was brought by a policeman to the courtroom for arraignment. Because he was escorted in this manner, it appears that he had no freedom of movement and, therefore, suffered an actual loss of liberty.

Deft negotiated a plea bargain with the prosecutor under which Deft agreed to enter a plea of guilty without admitting that he was, in fact, guilty. In exchange, the State would not request a jail term. The plea was explained to the court. The judge advised Deft of his constitutional rights that would be waived by the plea. These facts infer that Deft was advised that he was waiving his rights to counsel and that he understood the impact of doing so.

The judge explained to Deft that the plea arrangement did not limit the court's discretion in imposing the sentence. Deft then waived his rights and agreed to go forward with the plea. The judge accepted the plea and sentenced Deft to a fine of $500 and a 30 day suspended jail term. Although jail time was a possibility as explained by the judge, the jail term was suspended at time of sentencing. Absent the imposition of actual imprisonment, Deft has no right to appointed counsel. However, since Deft received a suspended sentence, counsel must be provided.

Deft's request for appointed counsel was improperly denied. The appellate court should rule that his Sixth Amendment right to counsel has been violated.

2. Denial of Right to a Trial by Jury

Sixth Amendment

The Sixth Amendment, applicable to the states through the Fourteenth Amendment, guarantees a trial by jury where a serious offense is charged with a potential sentence over six months.

Deft was formally charged with a criminal offense. Since the facts stipulate it was a criminal offense, it can be inferred that the offense was serious. This is, perhaps, why Deft was concerned enough to request a trial by jury.

Still, the offense was punishable with a 90 day maximum jail term and/or a $500 fine. The charged offense, by its own terms, did not carry a potential jail sentence over six months.

Deft's request for a jury trial was properly denied. The appellate court should rule that his Sixth Amendment right to a trial by jury has not been violated.

3. Any Identification Inadmissible At Trial

Sixth Amendment - Arraignment Identification

A police lineup or other face-to-face confrontation conducted after the accused has been formally charged with a crime is considered a critical stage of the proceedings and the accused has a right to have counsel present.

As Deft was being brought by a policeman to the courtroom for arraignment, Witt, who witnessed the charged offense and was asked by the prosecutor to be present at Deft's arraignment, said to the policeman, "Yes, that's the guy." It appears that Deft was being subjected to a face-to-face "show-up" identification at the direction of the prosecutor. Further, Deft had been formally charged with a criminal offense. Deft will argue that this was a critical stage in the proceedings during which he had a right to have counsel present.

It appears a Sixth Amendment violation occurred.

Due Process

Due process in an identification procedure will be violated only when the procedure is unreliable.

Deft was being brought to the courtroom where the arraignment was to take place. Witt had been instructed to come to the same courtroom. No other suspects were present. The "show-up" identification centered on Deft alone and might be considered unreliable and unnecessarily suggestive.

Therefore, the court ruled properly when it agreed to exclude evidence of Witt's statement to the policeman.

Fifth Amendment - Court Trial Identification

An in-court identification of the accused does not violate the accused's right to be free from self-incrimination.

The prosecution was apparently planning to use Witt at time of trial to identify Deft as the perpetrator of the crime for which he was being prosecuted. Allowing Witt to observe Deft during the court proceeding for purposes of in-court identification may be deemed a seizure of physical incriminating evidence from the defendant. However, the fifth amendment applies only to testimony that has been compelled from the lips of the defendant himself. It does not apply to evidence based on a witness's observation of the defendant at time of trial.

The court properly refused Deft's motion to prevent identification of Deft by Witt at trial. The appellate court should rule that Deft's Fifth Amendment rights have not been violated.

Sixth Amendment - Court Trial Identification

If a witness can identify the accused at the trial independently without having to rely on an earlier lineup identification, the in-court identification will be admissible.

Witt witnessed the offense that Deft was accused of committing. It appears that Witt had a sufficient opportunity to view Deft at the time of the crime. This alone would enable him to independently identify Deft at time of trial. There is no indication that Witt would have to rely on his previous inadmissible arraignment identification in order to make an independent in-court identification at time of trial.

If Deft was afforded his right to a speedy trial, the length of time between the crime and the identification would have been short. Based on the totality of circumstances, Witt's anticipated testimony would be purged of any primary taint related to the prior identification. Witt's in-court identification would be deemed reliable and admissible.

The court properly refused Deft's motion to prevent any potential identification of Deft by Witt at trial. The appellate court should rule that Deft's Sixth Amendment rights have not been violated.

4. Ineffective Guilty Plea

Sixth Amendment - Right To A Fair Trial

The Sixth Amendment guarantees an accused the right to a fair and impartial trial.

Deft negotiated a plea bargain. The judge advised him of the constitutional rights he would waive by pleading guilty. Deft then waived his rights and agreed to go forward with the plea. Although the accused is entitled to a fair and impartial trial, he can waive his rights. Based on the foregoing facts, Deft was aware that he could exercise his right to convene a jury trial but he choose to waive his right. The fact that he told the judge that he was really innocent does not taint his decision.

The appellate court should rule that Deft's rights were not violated when he waived his right to a trial.

Acceptance of A Guilty Plea

When accepting an accused's plea of guilty, the court must address the defendant personally in open court on the record to determine that the plea is voluntary and intelligent.

After Deft negotiated his plea bargain with the prosecutor under which he agreed to enter a plea of guilty without admitting that he was, in fact guilty, and the State agreed that it would not request jail time, the plea was explained to the court. The judge then advised Deft of the constitutional rights he would waive by pleading guilty. He also told Deft of the maximum statutory penalty that could be imposed. Deft waived his rights and agreed to go forward with his plea. By its instruction to Deft in open court and on the record, the court advised Deft of the nature of the charge, the maximum penalty possible, the fact that he had the right to plead not guilty and the fact that by pleading guilty, he waived his right to a jury trial. The Court's explanation was sufficient to ensure that Deft knew of and understood the charges. Therefore, Deft's decision to enter his plea was voluntary.

Moreover, the judge told Deft of the maximum statutory penalty that could be imposed explaining that the plea did not limit the court's discretion in imposing the maximum statutory penalty. Despite Deft's prior agreement with the prosecution, he understood the consequences of entering a guilty plea even though he maintained that he was innocent. The instruction given by the judge was sufficient to give Deft a reasonable basis upon which to understand the consequences of the plea bargain. By waiving his rights, authorizing the prosecutor to make a proffer of evidence to establish a factual basis for the charge and then entering his plea, Deft exercised his right to make an intelligent decision concerning his guilty plea.

The Court properly accepted Deft's guilty plea. The appellate Court should rule that his conviction should not be reversed.

CRIMINAL PROCEDURE/CRIMINAL LAW QUESTION #4

STATE v. DOUG

Doug was watching television in his ground floor apartment. When outside noise made it difficult to hear the sound, he looked out and saw a party in progress on the lawn. Doug yelled at the party-goers to be quiet and threw an empty bottle at them. The bottle hit a woman on the leg. Her boyfriend, Tom, ran to Doug's apartment, broke down the door, and approached Doug shaking his fist. Doug, who had been drinking heavily, reached into a drawer, removed a pistol, and immediately shot and killed Tom.

Doug fled, but was stopped the next day at the boarding gate of a publicly operated inter-city bus terminal when the pistol, which was in his pocket, activated a metal detector. The privately owned bus company had instituted the boarding procedure because it had been the object of several bomb threats in the preceding weeks.

Security personnel of the bus company detained Doug. Because they had read of Tom's death, and the pistol Doug was carrying was of the same caliber as that believed to have been used in the homicide, they seized the pistol. They released Doug. Later that day, they took the pistol to the police and told the police why they had taken it from Doug.

Thereafter, Doug was arrested on a city street by police officers on a charge of carrying a concealed weapon. The arresting officers told him that ballistics tests had proved his pistol had fired the bullets which killed Tom. Doug then blurted out, "I shot Tom in self-defense."

Doug has been charged with murder.

1. What objections based on the United States Constitution should Doug make to admission of the gun into evidence at trial and his statement? Discuss.

2. Assuming that all of the above facts are proved by competent evidence at trial, may Doug properly be convicted of first degree murder, or of any lesser included offenses, and if so, what offenses? Discuss.

IRAC OUTLINE SHEET

(I)	(R)	(A)	(C)

EXAMPLE OF PROPER IRAC OUTLINE

STATE v. DOUG

1. (A) DOUG'S (D) OBJECTIONS TO ADMISSION OF GUN:

(I)	(R)	(A)	(C)
4TH AMENDMENT	Protects Against Unreasonable Search/Seizure	Security personnel of bus co. detained D/seized pistol without a warrant	Violation
	Governmental Intrusion	D was stopped at the boarding gate of a publicly operated inter-city bus terminal Privately owned bus co. had instituted the boarding procedure because it had been the object of several bomb threats in preceding weeks Security personnel of bus co. detained/seized Took pistol to police	
	Expectation Of Privacy	Pistol in D's pocket	
EXCEPTIONS TO WARRANTLESS SEARCH:			
AIRPORT/BUS EXCEPTION	Public Policy	At boarding gate of bus terminal, the pistol activated metal detector The privately owned bus co. had instituted boarding procedure because it had been the object of several bomb threats in preceding weeks	Valid Exception
	No Probable Cause Required	No probable cause	
	No Consent Required	D fled/stopped at boarding gate at bus terminal when pistol activated metal detector	
STOP & FRISK	Reasonable Suspicion Crime	Pistol in D's pocket activated metal detector	Valid Exception
	Articulable Facts	Previous bomb threats supra	
	Stop	Detained	
	Pat Down For Weapons	Seized pistol	
EXIGENT CIRCUMSTANCES	Hot Pursuit Of Suspect	D shot/killed T/D fled	Valid Exception
	Loss/Destruction Of Evidence	Metal detector activated supra Security read of T's death/caliber pistol D carrying as that believed used in homicide	

1. (B) DOUG'S (D) OBJECTIONS TO ADMISSION OF STATEMENT "I SHOT TOM IN SELF-DEFENSE":

(I)	(R)	(A)	(C)
VALIDITY OF ARREST	Warrant Or Probable Cause	Security personnel detained D They read of T's death & pistol D carrying same caliber believed used in homicide/seized pistol They took pistol to police/told police why they had taken it from D D arrested on city street by police on charge of carrying a concealed weapon	Valid Arrest
5TH AMENDMENT	Custodial Interrogation	Arrested on street (no freedom of movement) Arresting officers told D that ballistics tests proved D's pistol had fired bullets which killed T (eliciting an incriminating response?) Doug blurted out "I shot T in self defense" (spontaneous declaration?)	Violation

(I)	(R)	(A)	(C)
STANDING	Common Law: Proprietary/Possessory Right	D's statement supra	Standing
	Modern Law: Reasonable Expectation Of Privacy Totality Of Circumstances	D's statement supra	
EXCLUSIONARY RULE	Evidence Of Illegal Search Inadmissible	Interrogation supra	Statement Inadmissible
	Fruit Of Poisonous Tree	Without a warrant D's statement to police	

2. STATE v. DOUG - MURDER:

(I)	(R)	(A)	(C)
HOMICIDE	Killing Of Another	D shot & killed T	Homicide
	Causation Actual	D shot & killed T (but for)	
	Proximate	D shot & killed T (foreseeable)	
MURDER	Unlawful Killing Of Another	D shot & killed T	Murder
	Malice Specific Intent to Kill	D reached into drawer, removed a pistol, & immediately shot Tom	
	Specific Intent To Cause Serious Bodily Harm	Shot T	
	Willful/Wanton Conduct	Shot T	
FIRST DEGREE MURDER	Specific Intent To Kill Plus	Shot T	No First Degree Murder
	Premeditation/Deliberation	Immediately shot T	
SECOND DEGREE MURDER	All Murder Not First Degree	Shot T	Second Degree Murder
EXCUSE: VOLUNTARY INTOXICATION	Negates Specific Intent	D had been drinking heavily	Invalid Excuse
JUSTIFICATION: SELF-DEFENSE	Deadly Force	D reached into drawer/ removed pistol/shot & killed T	Invalid Justification
	Reasonable Belief Of Deadly Attack	T ran to D's apt. broke down door/ approached D shaking his fist Threw bottle at T's girlfriend/ hit her on leg	
JUSTIFICATION: DEFENSE OF PROPERTY	Deadly Force	T ran to D's apt, broke down door/ approached shaking fist	Invalid Justification
	Protect Home	D's apartment	
VOLUNTARY MANSLAUGHTER	Murder	Supra	Voluntary Manslaughter
	Mitigation - Provocation	D watching T.V. Outside noise made it difficult to hear Looked out/saw party on lawn Yelled at party goers to be quiet & threw bottle at them T broke down door shaking fist D shot T immediately	
	Mitigation - Imperfect Defenses	Self defense/defense of property supra	

EXAMPLE OF IRAC CRIMINAL PROCEDURE ISSUE

(I) **Stop and Frisk**

(R) The Supreme Court, in Terry v. Ohio, found that where an officer has (1) a reasonable suspicion that a crime has been committed or is about to be committed based on (2) articulable facts, he may (3) stop a suspected felon and (4) conduct a pat down for weapons.

(A) The State may argue that when the pistol in Doug's pocket activated the metal detector, the security personnel had (1) a reasonable suspicion of criminal activity. Bomb threats in the preceding weeks formed the basis for (2) articulable facts giving the security personnel the right to (3) stop and detain Doug, (4) pat him down, and seize the pistol when it was felt.

(C) If, in fact, he was frisked prior to the seizure of the pistol, the seizure of Doug's pistol and its admissibility appear appropriate under the stop and frisk exception.

SUGGESTED MODEL ANSWER

STATE v. DOUG

1(A) DOUG'S OBJECTIONS TO ADMISSION OF GUN:

Fourth Amendment

The Fourth Amendment, applicable to the states through the Fourteenth Amendment, protects against unreasonable searches and seizures by a governmental intrusion upon a reasonable expectation of privacy.

When the security personnel of the bus company detained Doug and seized his pistol, they had no warrant. Their failure to obtain a warrant prior to the detention and seizure indicates that they conducted an unreasonable search and seizure.

Doug was stopped at the boarding gate of a publicly operated inter-city bus terminal. It was conducted by the bus company's security personnel who were employees of the privately owned bus company. Since they were acting to protect the public against bomb threats received in preceding weeks, their actions are sufficient to show a governmental intrusion.

The State will counter that the security personnel were private bus company agents acting on the sole instructions of their employer. They were not deputized. Therefore, they would not qualify as government agents sufficient for a governmental intrusion.

However, the duty of the security personnel was to protect the patrons of the publicly operated inter-city bus terminal from bomb threats. They were acting in a quasi-police function. Their conduct of detaining Doug, seizing the gun, and taking it to the police with a report of their conclusions will qualify as a governmental intrusion.

The pistol was taken from Doug's pocket. One normally has a reasonable expectation of privacy in his clothes and the objects contained therein.

Therefore, the search and seizure of the pistol falls within the Fourth Amendment. Since it was conducted without a warrant, it is presumed invalid unless the state can show an applicable exception.

Exceptions To Warrantless Search

Airport/Bus Exception

Public policy permits the warrantless search of persons boarding public transportation without probable cause or upon a showing of consent.

At the boarding gate of the publicly-operated inter-city bus terminal, the pistol in Doug's pocket activated the metal detector. This gave the security personnel a reasonable suspicion that Doug might be carrying a weapon. The desire to protect the traveling public from dangerous weapons is a sufficiently important public interest to justify the warrantless search of Doug's pocket and the seizure of the pistol.

Since the boarding procedure requiring passengers to go through the metal detector was a result of several bomb threats in preceding weeks, public policy will permit such a seizure without a further showing of probable cause.

Furthermore, Doug fled to the bus terminal where he stopped at the boarding gate. He voluntarily went to the area where the metal detector was located. Such conduct implies his consent to the search if the metal detector activated.

Therefore, the gun is admissible under this public policy exception to the Fourth Amendment.

Stop and Frisk

The Supreme Court, in Terry v. Ohio, found that where an officer has a reasonable suspicion that a crime has been committed or is about to be committed based on articulable facts, he may stop a suspected felon and conduct a pat down for weapons.

The State may argue that when the pistol in Doug's pocket activated the metal detector, the security personnel had a reasonable suspicion of criminal activity. Bomb threats in the preceding weeks formed the basis for articulable facts giving the security personnel the right to stop and detain Doug, pat him down, and seize the pistol when it was felt.

If, in fact, he was frisked prior to the seizure of the pistol, the seizure of Doug's pistol and its admissibility appear appropriate under the stop and frisk exception.

Exigent Circumstances

A warrantless search may be conducted when officers are in hot pursuit of a suspect or when the delay caused by obtaining a warrant would permit evidence to be lost or destroyed.

Doug fled from his home after he shot and killed Tom. The security personnel had read of Tom's death, witnessed the metal detector activation and believed that the gun seized from Doug matched the caliber of the pistol used in the crime. In order to prevent Doug from boarding the bus and fleeing, they had no time to obtain a warrant for arrest. To delay would have allowed Doug's escape onto the bus. Their conduct is a reasonably necessary response to the hot pursuit of a suspect.

Moreover, the security personnel heard the metal detector activate giving them probable cause to believe that contraband would be seized if the search was conducted without delay. Due to the potential loss or destruction of the evidence, the security personnel had little choice but to conduct the search without a warrant.

It appears that exigent circumstances will be a valid exception to the Fourth Amendment. Therefore, the gun is admissible.

1(B) DOUG'S OBJECTIONS TO ADMISSION OF STATEMENT, "I SHOT TOM IN SELF-DEFENSE":

Fourth Amendment - Validity Of Arrest

Under the Fourth Amendment, an officer may make a valid arrest when he has a warrant for arrest or has probable cause for the arrest based on a reasonable belief that a crime has been committed and that the arrestee committed it.

The facts do not indicate that the police had a warrant to arrest Doug. However, the bus company security personnel who had taken the gun seized from Doug had turned it over to them and had told them why it had been taken from Doug. Because the caliber of Doug's pistol was that believed to have been used in Tom's homicide, this information gave the police the reasonable belief that Tom's murder had been committed by Doug. On the basis of the information given by the security personnel, the State could establish probable cause to arrest Doug for carrying a concealed weapon, the charge upon which he was arrested.

The arrest is valid under the Fourth Amendment.

Fifth Amendment - Miranda

The police must inform the defendant of his right against self-incrimination prior to any custodial interrogation.

Doug was arrested on the street. Because he had no freedom of movement, he was in custody. The facts do not indicate that Doug was informed of his Miranda rights either before or after his arrest. Doug's statement was made subsequent to his arrest.

Doug will contend that his statement was made after the arresting officers told him that the ballistics tests proved his pistol fired the bullets that killed Tom. As such, he was the focus of the investigation. The police officers' comments constituted the functional equivalent of a custodial interrogation. Thus, he should have been Mirandized before the statement was made.

However, the State will rebut that Doug blurted out this statement in the absence of coercion. His blurt out constitutes a spontaneous declaration for which Miranda rights do not attach.

Under Rhode Island v. Innis, an officer who elicits an incriminating response during interrogation without first advising the defendant of his rights has violated Miranda.

The arresting officer told Doug that the ballistics test proved his gun killed Tom. This remark instigated his blurt out. The officer was, in fact, attempting to elicit such an incriminating response and did so before advising Doug of his right to remain silent.

The statement was the functional equivalent of a custodial interrogation and, therefore, violates Doug's Fifth Amendment protection against self-incrimination.

Standing To Invoke The Exclusionary Rule

At common law, the party seeking to exclude evidence must have a proprietary or possessory right in the evidence seized. Modernly, the court will examine the claimant's reasonable expectation of privacy under the totality of the circumstances.

Doug will argue that the statement sought to be suppressed was his own. Doug has both a proprietary and possessory right in his statements.

Based on the same facts, Doug will show that he had a reasonable expectation of privacy concerning the manner in which statements are taken from him by the police. Thus, based on the totality of the circumstances, Doug has standing to assert the exclusionary rule.

Exclusionary Rule

Pursuant to the Wong Sun case, evidence illegally obtained is inadmissible as a fruit of the poisonous tree.

Doug can establish that his statement was illegally obtained by means of an unlawful interrogation. Therefore, his statement to the police is a fruit of the poisonous tree and should be excluded.

In such case, the exclusionary rule will apply.

2. STATE v. DOUG - MURDER:

Homicide

Homicide is the killing of one human being by another human being.

Doug shot Tom who died. These facts demonstrate the killing of a human being by another human being.

Actual Causation

"But for" Doug shooting Tom, Tom would not have been killed. Doug is the actual cause of Tom's death.

Proximate Causation

Since Tom's death was the direct and foreseeable result of Doug's gunshot, Doug is the proximate cause of Tom's death.

It appears that Doug committed a homicide.

Murder

Murder is an unlawful killing committed with malice aforethought.

The facts indicate that Doug reached into a drawer, removed a pistol and immediately shot Tom to death. Thus, an unlawful killing occurred. The act of pointing and firing a deadly weapon at someone indicates an intent to kill or, at a minimum, the intent to cause serious bodily harm sufficient for malice.

The use of such a dangerous instrumentality in reckless disregard for Tom's life further indicates Doug's malignant heart which equates to willful, wanton conduct. These man endangering states of mind demonstrate a clear showing of malice.

Doug may be convicted of murder.

First Degree Murder

First degree murder is one committed with the specific intent to kill plus premeditation and deliberation.

As set forth above, Doug had the requisite specific intent to kill. Further, Doug reached into the drawer and removed the pistol stored there. He made the conscious decision to shoot and kill Tom, an act sufficient to prove premeditation.

However, the facts indicate that after Tom broke down Doug's door, Doug "immediately shot" Tom. Doug will argue that he had no time to contemplate and appreciate the consequences of his act. It appears from the facts that Doug acted instinctively and had no time to deliberate his act.

Therefore, he may not be convicted of first degree murder.

Second Degree Murder

Second degree murder is all murder that is not first degree.

If Doug is found not guilty of first degree murder, he will be found guilty of second degree murder.

Excuse: Voluntary Intoxication

Voluntary intoxication is not an excuse to murder but may be used to negate specific intent.

The facts indicate that Doug had been drinking heavily indicating that he was voluntarily intoxicated. Doug may invoke this excuse to negate a first degree murder charge based on specific intent to kill. However, due to lack of premeditation on and deliberation, supra, first degree is doubtful.

Therefore, his intoxication will not excuse a charge of murder in the second degree.

Justification: Self-Defense

One may defend himself with deadly force where he has a reasonable belief that he is being subjected to a deadly attack.

The facts indicate that Doug reached into the drawer and removed a pistol and shot Tom. Doug's use of deadly force appears justified because Tom broke down his door and approached Doug shaking his fist. Doug was in fear for his life and had a reasonable belief that he was under a deadly attack.

The State will rebut that Doug was the aggressor in the fight. He started the incident when he threw the bottle at Tom's girlfriend hitting her on the leg. Further, as he approached Doug, Tom was merely shaking his fist. As such, Doug was being subjected to a non-deadly threat. He was not justified by responding with the deadly force of a pistol.

It appears that Doug used excessive force. He cannot claim a justification of self-defense.

Justification: Defense Of Property

One has a right to use deadly force to protect one's home.

Doug will contend that when Tom ran to Doug's apartment and broke down his door shaking his fist, he had a right to protect his "home" with deadly force.

Nonetheless, the degree of force used by Doug was more than that necessary to protect his home. Tom was not armed with a weapon. He was apparently not posing a dangerous threat to Doug or the property by the mere shaking of his fist.

It appears that Doug used excessive force. He cannot claim a justification of defense of property.

Voluntary Manslaughter

Voluntary manslaughter is a killing that would otherwise be murder but for some legally recognized form of mitigation.

Adequate Provocation

Doug will assert that he was watching television. He was provoked into using deadly force by the noise of the outside party that made it difficult for him to hear it. When he looked out and saw the party in progress on the lawn, it so angered him that he yelled at the party goers to be quiet. He resorted to throwing a bottle to try to quiet the party. He was further provoked when Tom broke down his door and approached him shaking his fist.

When Tom approached him after breaking down the door, Doug shot Tom immediately, killing him. He had no time to cool off before the shooting. Thus, Tom's murder should be mitigated.

However, the State will successfully argue that Tom's actions in conjunction with the loud party provoked nothing more than a fist fight.

No adequate provocation existed sufficient to mitigate a charge of murder to voluntary manslaughter.

Imperfect Defenses

Voluntary manslaughter is a killing that would otherwise be murder but for some legally recognized form of mitigation.

As set forth above, Doug's defenses will not justify his crime under the circumstances. However, such would suffice as imperfect defenses which may legally act to mitigate a charge of murder in the second degree to voluntary manslaughter.

Based on the foregoing, Doug should be convicted of voluntary manslaughter.

CRIMINAL PROCEDURE/CRIMINAL LAW QUESTION #5

MIKE AND DAN

Just before closing time Mike and Dan entered the Shorecliff Pharmacy to steal money and narcotics. While Mike ransacked the store, Dan took the proprietor, Fred, outside. As Dan pistol whipped Fred to learn the location of valuables, his gun accidentally discharged, wounding Fred. Dan fled. Mike came out and saw Fred's bleeding body. Thinking Fred was dying, Mike pushed him over a nearby cliff, and drove away at high speed. Fred's gunshot wound was not serious, but he died from injuries sustained in the fall. A neighbor called police and reported that he had heard a gunshot and had seen a car speed away from the pharmacy.

Police immediately set up a roadblock at which Mike's car was stopped. When an officer asked Mike to leave the car, Mike hesitated. The officer then reached into Mike's bulging pocket and pulled out a gun. Mike was given Miranda advice and taken to the police station. The next day Mike's car was towed to the station and searched. Under the front seat, police found a "Shorecliff" envelope filled with drugs. When they showed the envelope to Mike he immediately blurted out: "Dan was the one who shot the guy who was bleeding to death."

Mike and Dan were indicted for the murder of Fred. Separate trials were ordered at the request of each defendant.

(1) On appropriate motion, which of the following items of evidence should be excluded or suppressed at the trial of Dan:

(a) the gun taken from Mike's pocket:

(b) the Shorecliff envelope and contents taken from Mike's car:

(c) Mike's extrajudicial statement.

Discuss.

(2) Assuming all the facts stated are proven by proper evidence, may Mike properly be convicted of the murder of Fred and, if so, in what degree? Discuss.

(3) Assuming all the facts stated are proven by proper evidence, may Dan properly be convicted of the murder of Fred and, if so, in what degree'? Discuss.

IRAC OUTLINE SHEET

(I)	(R)	(A)	(C)

EXAMPLE OF PROPER IRAC OUTLINE

STATE v. DAN

1. SHOULD FOLLOWING ITEMS BE SUPPRESSED AT DAN'S (D) TRIAL:

(a) GUN IN MIKE'S (M) POCKET:

(I)	(R)	(A)	(C)
PROBABLE CAUSE TO INVESTIGATE (ROADBLOCK)	Reasonable Belief Dangerous Crime	Neighbor called police Reported he heard a gunshot & had seen a car Committed speed away from the pharmacy (private citizen presumed reliable)	Probable Cause To Investigate
	Person Stopped Committed The Crime	Police immediately set up roadblock at which M's car was stopped When officer asked M to leave the car, M hesitated	
4th AMENDMENT	Protects Against Unreasonable Searches/Seizure	Officer reached into M's bulging pocket/pulled out gun without a warrant	Arguable Violation
	Governmental Intrusion	Police officer	
	Expectation Of Privacy	M's pocket?	
EXCEPTIONS TO WARRANTLESS SEARCH:			
STOP & FRISK	Reasonable Suspicion Crime	Neighbor's call (supra)	Invalid Exception
	Articulable Facts	Car sped away from crime scene	
	Stop	M's car stopped	
	Pat Down For Weapons	Officer asked M to leave car M hesitated supra Officer reached into M's bulging pocket	
STANDING	Common Law: Proprietary/Possessory Right	M's car/gun in M's pocket	No Standing Gun Admissible
	Modern Law: Reasonable Expectation Of Privacy Totality Of Circumstances	M's car/gun in M's pocket	

(b) SHORECLIFF ENVELOPE & ITS CONTENTS:

(I)	(R)	(A)	(C)
4th AMENDMENT	Protects Against Unreasonable Searches/Seizures	The next day, M's car towed to station searched without a warrant/under front seat police found Shorecliff envelope filled with drugs	Arguable Violation
	Governmental Intrusion	Police	
	Expectation Of Privacy	M's car?	
EXCEPTION TO WARRANTLESS SEARCH:			
SEARCH INCIDENT TO ARREST	Valid Arrest	M given Miranda advise & taken to police station	Invalid Exception
	Search In Immediate Control	The next day car towed & searched	
	Contemporaneous	Under the front seat of car police found supra	
AUTOMOBILE EXCEPTION	Mobility	M's car The next day supra	Invalid Exception
	Probable Cause	No facts	

(I)	(R)	(A)	(C)
IMPOUNDMENT/ INVENTORY SEARCH	Auto	M's car	Invalid Exception
	Lawful Impoundment	The next day M's car towed to police station & searched	
	Inventory To Protect Defendant's Possessions & Police From Theft Allegations	The next day, car searched Under front seat the police found envelope supra (standard operating procedure?)	
STANDING	Common Law: Proprietary/Possessory Right	M's car/envelope filled with drugs	Arguable Standing
	Modern Law: Reasonable Expectation Of Privacy Totality Of Circumstances	M's car/envelope filled with drugs	
EXCLUSIONARY RULE	Evidence Of Illegal Search Inadmissible	Search of car supra No warrant	Arguably Applicable
	Fruit Of Poisonous Tree	Drugs	

(c) MIKE'S EXTRAJUDICIAL STATEMENT:

(I)	(R)	(A)	(C)
5th AMENDMENT	Custodial Interrogation	M given Miranda advice & taken to police station Police showed envelope to M (elicit incriminating response?) M immediately blurted out D was the one who shot the guy	Arguable Violation
STANDING	No Standing To Exclude Third Party Statements	M immediately blurted out supra	No Standing
HEARSAY	Out-Of-Court Statement	Statement made at police station	Hearsay
	Truth Of Matter Asserted	D was the one who shot the guy supra	
EXCEPTION: ADMISSION STATEMENT OF A CO-CONSPIRATOR	Conspiracy Independently Established	M & D entered the Pharmacy to steal money & narcotics	Inadmissible
	Statement Made During Conspiracy	Statement made at police station next day after Arrest supra	
	Statement Made In Furtherance Of Conspiracy	Statement made at police station supra	

STATE v. MIKE (M)

(2) MAY M BE CONVICTED OF MURDER, WHAT DEGREE?:

(I)	(R)	(A)	(C)
HOMICIDE	Killing Of Another	M pushed F over a nearby cliff F died from injuries sustained in the fall	Homicide
	Causation Actual	Fs gunshot wound was not serious M pushed F over nearby cliff (but for)	
	Proximate	Thinking he was dying, M pushed F F died from injuries sustained in the fall	
MURDER	Unlawful Killing Of Another	Supra	Murder
	Malice Specific Intent To Kill	Thinking F was dying, M pushed him off the cliff	
	Specific Intent To Cause Serious Bodily Harm	Thinking F was dying, M pushed him off the cliff	
	Felony Murder	M & D entered pharmacy to steal	
	Common Law Burglary: Breaking	Just before closing, entered to steal narcotics/money	No C/L Burglary

(I)	(R)	(A)	(C)
	Entering	Entered	
	Dwelling House Of Another	Pharmacy	
	Nighttime	Just before closing	
	Specific Intent To Commit Felony Therein	To steal	
	M/L Burglary		M/L Burglary
	Unlawful Entrance	Entered pharmacy to steal	
	Structure	Pharmacy	
	Intent To Commit A Crime	To steal money/narcotics	
	Robbery:		
	Trespassory Taking	M ransacked the store	
	Carrying Away	Ransacked store	
	Personal Properly Of Another	Drugs	
	Force Or Fear	Pistol whipped	
	Intent To Permanently Deprive	Steal	
<u>FIRST DEGREE MURDER</u>	Specific Intent To Kill Plus	Pushed F supra	First Degree Murder
	Premeditation/Deliberation	Thinking F was dying threw him off nearby cliff	
	Felony Murder	Burglary/robbery supra	

<u>STATE v. DAN (Note: Some Students May Handle As Accomplice Liability, If So, Ok)</u>

(3) <u>MAY DAN (D) BE CONVICTED OF MURDER, WHAT DEGREE</u>?

(I)	(R)	(A)	(C)
<u>HOMICIDE</u>	Killing Of Another	M pushed him over cliff F died from injuries sustained in the fall	Homicide
	Causation		
	Actual	D pistol whipped F Gun accidentally discharged wounding F Gunshot not serious M pushed him over the cliff (substantial factor?)	
	Proximate	Pistol whipped supra M pushed F supra (M's act intervening?)	
<u>MURDER</u>	Unlawful Killing Of Another	Supra	Murder
	Malice		
	Specific Intent To Kill	Gun accidentally discharged	
	Specific Intent To Cause Serious Bodily Harm	Pistol whipped	
	Wanton Conduct	Pistol whipped	
	Felony Murder	Burglary/robbery supra	
<u>FIRST DEGREE</u>	Felony Murder	Burglary/robbery supra	First Degree Murder

EXAMPLE OF IRAC CRIMINAL PROCEDURE ISSUE

(I) **Exceptions to Warrantless Search - Search Incident to Arrest**

(R) The police, pursuant to a (1) valid arrest, may (2) search the area within the immediate control of the defendant provided the search is (3) contemporaneous with the arrest.

(A) The facts are silent as to whether Mike was arrested. However, since Mike was Mirandized, a (1) valid arrest may be assumed. The search under the front seat of the car was conducted at the police station one day after Mike was arrested. Therefore, the (2) search was not in an area within the immediate control of the defendant nor was it (3) contemporaneous with the arrest.

(C) The search was invalid as a search incident to arrest.

SUGGESTED MODEL ANSWER

STATE v. DAN

(1) SHOULD FOLLOWING ITEMS BE SUPPRESSED AT TRIAL:

(a) GUN IN MIKE'S POCKET:

Probable Cause to Investigate Roadblock

The police may stop individuals and establish a roadblock if they have a reasonable belief that a dangerous crime has been committed and that the person stopped committed the crime. If the police stop every car, no suspicion or cause is required.

The State will argue that a neighbor called the police and reported that he heard a gunshot and had seen a car speed away from the pharmacy. Since the courts have found that private informants can be reliable, and since there was corroboration, the police had a reasonable belief that a dangerous crime had been committed.

The police set up the roadblock immediately at which point Mike's car was stopped. The stop, coupled with Mike's hesitation to leave the car upon the officer's request, formed the basis for suspecting that Mike, the person stopped, may have been involved in the commission of a crime at the Shorecliff Pharmacy.

The police, therefore, had probable cause to stop Mike to investigate. The roadblock was legal.

Fourth Amendment

The Fourth Amendment, applicable to the states through the Fourteenth Amendment, protects against unreasonable searches and seizures by a governmental intrusion upon a reasonable expectation of privacy.

When the police officer reached into Mike's bulging pocket and pulled out the gun, he did so without a warrant. The officer's failure to obtain a warrant prior to the search and seizure of the gun indicates that he conducted an unreasonable search and seizure. The police officer took the gun as part of his official duties. His actions constitute a governmental intrusion. Finally, Mike's pocket was the object of the search. One normally has an expectation of privacy in one's pocket and the objects contained therein.

However, since it was Mike's pocket, it is doubtful whether Dan would have an expectation of privacy in the items found therein. If he can show he did, the police were bound to obtain a warrant before searching Mike.

Therefore, the search and seizure of the gun falls within the Fourth Amendment. Since it was conducted without a warrant, it is presumed invalid unless the State can show an applicable exception.

Exceptions to Warrantless Search

Stop and Frisk

The Supreme Court, in Terry v. Ohio, found that where an officer has a reasonable suspicion that a crime has been committed or is about to be committed based on articulable facts, he may stop a suspected felon and conduct a pat down for weapons.

Based upon the information from the neighbor, (supra), the police had reasonable suspicion that a crime had been committed. Since a car had been seen speeding away from the pharmacy, this formed the basis for articulable facts necessary to justify the stop of Mike's car.

Moreover, Mike' s hesitation to leave the car when requested to by the officer gave the police the right to conduct a pat down search of Mike at the roadblock site.

Still, it does not appear that Mike's hesitation without more created a reasonable belief that Mike was armed and dangerous. The police did not conduct a pat down for weapons. Rather, the officer reached into Mike's bulging pocket. This action exceeded the scope of a frisk.

Therefore, the gun was illegally obtained. The stop and frisk was invalid.

Standing to Invoke the Exclusionary Rule

At common law, the party seeking to exclude evidence must have a proprietary or possessory right in the evidence seized. Modenly, the court will examine the claimant's reasonable expectation of privacy under the totality of the circumstances.

The State will assert that the gun sought to be suppressed belonged to Mike, not to Dan. There are no facts to indicate Dan's ownership of the gun. Dan has no apparent proprietary or possessory right in the gun.

Modernly, the State will show that Dan lacked any legitimate interest in Mike's pocket or Mike's gun. Therefore, even under the more liberal interpretation of the reasonable expectation of privacy under the totality of the circumstances test, Dan has no standing to exclude the gun.

Therefore, the gun is admissible and should not be suppressed at Dan's trial.

(b) SHORECLIFF ENVELOPE AND ITS CONTENTS:

Fourth Amendment

Defined supra.

Mike's car was towed to the police station the next day after his arrest. The police searched under the front seat of the car where a Shorecliff envelope was found filled with drugs. Since no warrant was obtained prior to the search, the police conducted an unreasonable search and seizure. The police were acting in their law enforcement capacity. This action would be a governmental intrusion into Mike's car where he would have an expectation of privacy.

However, since it was Mike's car, it is doubtful whether Dan would also have an expectation of privacy there. If he can show that he would, the search and seizure of the gun is presumed invalid unless the state can show an applicable exception.

Exceptions to Warrantless Search

Search Incident to Arrest

The police, pursuant to a valid arrest, may search the area within the immediate control of the defendant provided the search is contemporaneous with the arrest.

The facts are silent as to whether Mike was arrested. Yet, since Mike was Mirandized, a valid arrest may be assumed. The search under the front seat of the car was conducted at the police station one day after Mike was arrested. Therefore, the search was not in an area within the immediate control of the defendant nor was it contemporaneous with the arrest.

The search was invalid as a search incident to arrest.

Automobile Exception

The courts have decided that the mobility of cars may justify an immediate search of the entire automobile provided there is probable cause to believe that contraband is in the car.

The State may argue that it had a right to immediately search the car because it could be moved before a warrant could be obtained.

However, Mike was in police custody and the car was not towed to the police station until the next day at which time it was searched at that location. The car was in no immediate danger of being moved. It is unlikely that it would be moved before a warrant could be obtained.

Further, the search was not conducted until one day after Mike's arrest. There was no probable cause to believe that the car contained contraband. If so, the car would have been searched immediately.

Therefore, the automobile exception will not apply as a valid exception.

Impoundment/Inventory Search

The police may search a automobile which is lawfully impounded to protect the defendant's possessions and to protect the police from theft allegations provided there are standard operating procedures so allowing.

Mike's automobile was towed to the police station. Because it was lawfully impounded, the police were justified in conducting an inventory search to protect Mike's possessions while he was in custody and to protect the police from theft allegations.

Nevertheless, the car was not searched until the following day. The facts do not indicate that standard operating procedures permitted the search. It was unlikely that the police were solely motivated by a desire to protect the defendant's possessions or themselves from theft allegations. If they had been, they would have impounded and inventoried the car on the same day that they arrested Mike. Therefore, the impoundment was unlawful and the subsequent search was invalid.

The impoundment/inventory exception will not be a valid exception to the Fourth Amendment. Thus, the envelope and its contents were illegally seized.

Standing to Invoke the Exclusionary Rule

Defined supra.

There are no facts to indicate that Dan was in the car at the time of the stop. Since the car belonged to Mike, it is unlikely that Dan could assert either a proprietary or possessory right in the drugs found therein.

However, if Dan is charged with robbery or burglary (infra), an important part of the State's case would involve the introduction of the drugs in the envelope. As such, the court would look to his reasonable expectation of privacy under the totality of circumstances test.

It is likely that Dan may have standing to exclude the envelope and its contents under modern law.

Dan may have standing to assert the exclusionary rule.

Exclusionary Rule

Defined supra.

The contents of the envelope were obtained as a result of an illegal warrantless search (supra). They should be inadmissible as fruits of the poisonous tree.

Dan could seek to exclude them under the Wong Sun ruling provided he could establish standing.

The exclusionary rule may apply.

(c) MIKE'S EXTRAJUDICIAL STATEMENT "DAN WAS THE ONE...."

Fifth Amendment- Miranda

The police must inform the defendant of his rights against self-incrimination prior to any custodial interrogation.

The State will contend that Mike was given Miranda advise at the time he was taken to the police station. Thus, Mike was informed of his rights against self-incrimination.

Further, Mike's statement that "Dan was the one who shot the guy who was bleeding the death," was made one day after Mike had been advised of his Miranda rights. Since Mike "blurted out" his statement, the police were under no obligation to re-Mirandize Mike. The statement was "immediate" giving them no time to do so.

Dan will counter that under Rhode Island v. Innis, an officer who elicits an incriminating response during interrogation without first advising the defendant of his rights has violated Miranda.

The statement was made only after the police showed Mike the envelope. At that time, he was the focus of the investigation. Thus, he should have been re-Mirandized before he was shown the envelope. The officers' failure to do so was a clear attempt by the police to elicit an incriminating response. Since Mike would not have made the statement absent this instigation by the officer, the action of the officer was the functional equivalent of a custodial interrogation.

The statement was illegally obtained in violation of the Fifth Amendment.

Standing

The general rule is that one has no standing under the Fifth Amendment to exclude the statements of third parties.

Since the statement was made by Mike, Dan has no standing to exclude Mike's illegally obtained statement. However, if Mike testifies, Dan would have a right to confront Mike as a witness against him.

Dan has no standing to exclude the extrajudicial statement.

Hearsay

An out-of-court statement offered to prove the truth of the matter asserted.

Dan will show that Mike's statement was made at the police station and was, therefore, an out-of-court statement. Since the statement is apparently being admitted to prove that Dan was the one who shot Fred, it appears that it is being offered to prove the truth of the matter asserted.

The statement is hearsay and will not be admitted unless the State can show an applicable exception.

Exception: Admission - Co-Conspirator Statements

Hearsay statements of a co-conspirator may be admitted if the conspiracy can be independently established, the statement was made during the conspiracy, and the statement was made in furtherance of the conspiracy.

Mike and Dan entered the Shorecliff Pharmacy to steal money and narcotics. These facts can be used to independently establish the conspiracy to steal.

The statement was made at the police station the next day after the crime was committed. Therefore, the conspiracy had ended. Thus, the statement was not made during the conspiracy or in furtherance of it.

The statement should he excluded as hearsay.

STATE v. MIKE - DEATH OF FRED

(2) MAY MIKE BE CONVICTED OF MURDER, IF SO WHAT DEGREE?

Homicide

Homicide is the killing of one human being by another human being.

Fred died after Mike pushed him off a nearby cliff. Thus, the facts demonstrate the killing of a human being by another human being.

Actual Causation

The gunshot wound Fred received from Dan was not serious. "But for" Mike pushing Fred over the nearby cliff, Fred would not have died. Mike is the actual cause of Fred's death

Proximate Causation

Fred died as a direct result of the injuries he sustained in the fall. Since Mike thought Fred was dying, it was foreseeable that Mike's actions would result in a quicker death. Thus, Mike is the proximate cause of the death.

It appears that Mike committed a homicide.

Murder

Murder is an unlawful killing of another committed with malice aforethought.

When Mike pushed Fred off the cliff, he thought Fred was dying from the gunshot wound. It can be argued that Mike's conduct was motivated by a desire to ensure that Fred would not be discovered and live to identify Mike and Dan. Thus, Mike committed an unlawful killing.

Since Mike hastened what he thought was imminent death by inflicting further serious bodily injuries when he pushed Fred off the cliff, Mike can be shown to have specifically intended to kill Fred, or, at a minimum, intended to cause serious bodily harm sufficient for malice.

The State will further attempt to show that Fred was killed while Mike was committing the dangerous felonies of burglary and/or robbery.

Common Law Burglary

Common law burglary is the breaking and entering of the dwelling house of another in the nighttime with the specific intent to commit a felony therein.

Just before closing time, Mike and Dan entered the Pharmacy to steal money and narcotics. Since their presence in the store was for unlawful purposes, their conduct constituted a trespassory breaking and entering. However, the Pharmacy is not a dwelling house. There are no facts to determine if it was nighttime. Although their specific intent was to steal, no common law burglary has been committed.

Modern Law Burglary

Modernly, a burglary is the unlawful entrance into a structure with the intent to commit a crime therein.

Mike and Dan entered the Pharmacy just before its closing time, not to buy, but to steal. This which would constitute an unlawful entrance. The Pharmacy is a structure. The intent has been previously established.

Thus, Mike and Dan committed a modern law burglary.

Robbery

Robbery is the trespassory taking and carrying away of the personal property of another by means of force or fear with the specific intent to permanently deprive.

The State will show that Mike and Dan ransacked the store and took drugs and money from Fred without consent establishing a trespassory taking and carrying away of the personal property of another. Pistol whipping Fred was the force they used to accomplish their task. Since they specifically intended to steal, permanent deprivation of the money and drugs is present.

Mike and Dan committed a robbery. Both felonies would be sufficient to establish malice for the felony murder rule.

Mike may be convicted of murder.

First Degree Murder

First degree murder is one committed with the specific intent to kill plus premeditation and deliberation or felony murder.

As established previously, Mike acted with the specific intent to kill.

The facts indicate that Mike threw Fred off a "nearby" cliff. It appears that Mike had to look for a place to dispose of Fred's body and then move Fred to the "nearby" cliff. The State will argue that during this time, Mike had an opportunity to contemplate and appreciate the consequences of his actions and make a conscious decision to act. The facts do not indicate an impulsive or instinctive act. Thus, it appears that Mike acted with the necessary premeditation and deliberation.

Further, since the State can establish that Fred was killed during the burglary or robbery (supra), it can obtain a first degree murder conviction against Mike under the felony murder rule.

It appears that Mike will be convicted of first degree murder.

STATE v. DAN - DEATH OF FRED

(3) MAY DAN BE CONVICTED OF MURDER, IF SO, WHAT DEGREE?

Homicide

As established previously, Fred died when Mike pushed him from the cliff. These facts demonstrate the killing of a human being by another human being.

Actual Causation

Dan will argue that the wounds Fred sustained from Dan's pistol whipping and accidental gunshot wound were not serious. The cause of Fred's death was the injuries he sustained in the fall off the cliff. Thus, there is not causal connection between the death of Fred and Dan's initial act.

The facts indicate that Mike threw Fred off the cliff because Fred thought he was dying from the gunshot wound inflicted by Dan. The State will argue that the combination of Dan's wounding Fred and Mike's pushing Fred off the cliff was a substantial factor in the death of Fred.

Therefore, Dan is the actual cause of Fred's death.

Proximate Causation

Dan only pistol whipped Fred. Fred's gunshot wound was not serious. Mike's act of throwing Fred off the cliff was an unforeseeable intervening act. Dan was, therefore, not the proximate cause of Fred's death. However, it is foreseeable that co-felons act in concert. Mike's act of "disposing of the body" was a foreseeable result of Dan's previous actions. Mike's act will not cut off Dan's liability.

Thus, a homicide has occurred.

Murder

Defined supra.

Dan will assert that his gun accidentally discharged. He did not have the necessary specific intent to kill. Thus, there was no unlawful killing. Still, the act of pistol whipping someone with a loaded gun demonstrates an intent to cause serious bodily harm. At a minimum, it is so grossly careless that it amounts to wanton conduct sufficient to establish malice.

Further, as previously discussed, the State may show that Fred's death occurred during the commission of the inherently dangerous felonies of burglary and robbery, thereby establishing malice under the felony murder rule.

First Degree Murder

Defined supra.

Since the State can establish the robbery and burglary, discussed supra, it will obtain a first degree murder conviction against Dan as a co-felon under the felony murder rule.

Therefore, Dan may be convicted of first degree murder.

SECTION VII

CORPORATIONS

CORPORATIONS

LEARN TO WRITE . . . THE RIGHT WAY®

IRAC OUTLINE SHEET

(I)	(R)	(A)	(C)

EXAMPLE OF PROPER IRAC OUTLINE

1. TED (T) v. JELCO (J)

(I)	(R)	(A)	(C)
PRE - INCORPORATION AGREEMENT	Agreement Between Promoter - 3rd Party	G entered into written contract with T $4,000 services for 6 months To commence 3 weeks later on behalf of J	Enforceable Agreement
	Prior To Incorporation	G signed contract by G on behalf of J a corporation to be formed	
	Corporate Acceptance	T worked in the jewelry sales business for J for 3 months w/o knowledge of any events occurring after his execution of the contract with G When T inquired about his compensation he discovered G had disappeared J refused to honor his contract	
DEFENSE CORPORATION BY ESTOPPEL	Defect In Incorporation Serious Enough To Deny Corporate Existence	G immediately prepared articles of incorporation for J In his haste, G failed to set forth purpose of corporation in articles as required by State X laws	Invalid Defense
	Corporation Deals With Third Person Estopped To Deny Its Validity	Despite omission, a charter was issued to J by State X after articles filed G/D/C held incorporators meeting in accordance with State X law/they were duly elected directors By unanimous vote, they accepted stock subscription J accepted T's services supra	

2. TED (T) v. CARL (C)/DAN (D)

(I)	(R)	(A)	(C)
DE JURE CORPORATION	Full/Substantial Compliance State Incorporation Laws	G prepared articles supra In his haste, failed to set forth purpose of corporation as required by State X laws	Invalid
DE FACTO CORPORATION	Good Faith Compliance With State Incorporation Laws	G failed to set forth purpose in articles in his haste to file supra Despite omission, a State X charter issued to J after articles filed	Valid
	Good Faith Exercise Corporate Powers	G/D/C held initial incorporators' meeting for J in accordance with State X law & they were duly elected directors By unanimous vote, the 3 directors then accepted the stock subscription of G/A/B Share certificates issued	
DEFENSE CORPORATION BY ESTOPPEL	Defect In Incorporation Serious Enough To Deny Corporate Existence	Supra	Valid Defense
	Individual Deals With Corp Entity Estopped To Deny Its Validity	G signed contract on behalf of J supra T worked 3 months supra T inquired about this compensation from J	

3. JELCO (J) v. ART/BOB (A/B)

(I)	(R)	(A)	(C)
PRE-INCORPORATION STOCK SUBSCRIPTION	Offer Corporate Stock	G/A/B met & orally agreed to pay $3,000 each for all J stock, a jewelry sales corp to be formed	Split Of Jurisdictions

(I)	(R)	(A)	(C)
	Requires Acceptance By Shareholder	Before anything further had been done, A/B wrote Gil & stated that they "hereby revoke any agreement to subscribe to the stock of any corporation to be formed by G" (majority/minority split) G wrote back "impossible to rescind" G/C/D held initial corporate meeting supra By unanimous vote, the 3 directors accepted G/A/B's stock subscription Neither A nor B attended the meeting	Valid Defense
	Consideration	Share certificates were issued to G/A/B Gil paid $3,000 for his shares A/B refused to pay or participate in J's business	
DEFENSE STATUTE OF FRAUDS	Writing Required	A State X statute provides "a contract for sale of securities is not enforceable unless there is a writing signed by party against whom enforcement is sought G/A/B met orally & agreed to purchase supra A & B wrote to G stating "revoke" supra G wrote back supra	Valid Defense
	Sale Securities	A/B/G agreed to pay $3,000 each for J stock	
ESTOPPEL (MINOR)	Detrimental Reliance By Promisor On Promisee's Words/Acts	G/AIB met & agreed to pay $3,000 each Issued shares to A/B Before anything further done, A/B wrote stating "revoke" supra G contracted with T a week earlier prior to agreement with A/B	Invalid

EXAMPLE OF IRAC CORPORATIONS ISSUE

(I) **Pre-Incorporation Stock Subscription**

(R) A pre-incorporation stock subscription is (1) an offer of corporate stock to potential shareholders requiring (2) acceptance and (3) consideration.

(A) Gil, Art and Bob met and orally agreed to each pay $3,000 for all of the Jelco stock. However, Jelco had not yet been formed. A majority of courts would hold such a pre-incorporation subscription unenforceable because the corporation was not yet in existence giving it no power to contract. Thus, the agreement was merely a (1) "continuing offer" to purchase the shares when Jelco came into existence.

When Art and Bob wrote Gil before anything further had been done stating that they "hereby revoke any agreement to subscribe to the stock of any corporation to be formed by Gil," no corporate acceptance had yet taken place. Art and Bob's revocation was valid.

In a minority of jurisdictions, Jelco would assert that Al and Bob's agreement to buy the stock was irrevocable. Allowing Art and Bob to revoke would work a hardship on Jelco. It would cause Jelco to be undercapitalized by $6,000. Gil affirmed this position by writing them that it was "impossible to rescind."

Further, by unanimous vote at the initial incorporator's meeting, Gil, Carl and Dan, the three Jelco directors, (2) accepted the stock subscriptions. Although neither Art nor Bob attended that meeting, share certificates were issued to all three. Gil paid $3,000 for his shares. Such conduct would be deemed Jelco's acceptance of Art and Bob's subscription offer to become shareholders upon the formation of the corporation. As such, Art and Bob's subscriptions were binding and irrevocable at the moment the subscription was made.

Thus, Art and Bob's refusal to pay the $3,000 (3) consideration for any stock or to participate in the business of Jelco would make them liable to Jelco and the other shareholders for any increased liability or loss which they bear as a result of the refusal. Jelco may recover the full subscription price from Art and Bob.

(C) Depending on the jurisdiction, so will determine the validity of the stock subscription.

SUGGESTED MODEL ANSWER

1. TED v. JELCO

Pre-Incorporation Agreement

A pre-incorporation agreement is an agreement between a promoter and a third party prior to incorporation which requires corporate acceptance.

Gil entered into a written contract with Ted "on behalf of Jelco, a corporation to be formed." It was agreed that Ted would be paid $4,000 for his services as a Jelco jewelry salesman for six months to commence in three weeks. Gil was Jelco's promoter who initiated the formation of the agreement between he and Ted, a third party. Since Jelco was yet to be formed, the contract was made prior to its incorporation.

Ted worked in the Jelco jewelry sales business for three months without knowledge of the events occurring after his execution of the contract with Gil. If he generated any business for Jelco during this time, it would be difficult for Jelco to argue that it was not on notice of Ted's services expended on its behalf. Since Jelco impliedly ratified Ted's three months of services, it, in effect, accepted his contract.

When Ted inquired about his compensation, he discovered Jelco's promoter, Gil, had disappeared. Thus, Jelco's refusal to honor Ted's contract was a breach of its pre-incorporation agreement.

Jelco will rebut that it did not become automatically bound by Gil's pre-incorporation contract with Ted. Since the Jelco board never approved the contract between Gil and Ted, Jelco is not bound and Gil would remain primarily liable for the contract absent evidence of a novation. However, since Gil had disappeared, if it is found that Jelco ratified the contract, Jelco would remain liable as a guarantor.

Ted may enforce his pre-incorporation agreement against Jelco.

Defense - Corporation by Estoppel

A defect in incorporation can be serious enough to deny an entity corporate existence. Nevertheless, a corporation who deals with a third person as if it is a corporation will be estopped to deny its validity as to its corporate obligations.

The facts indicate Gil immediately prepared the articles of incorporation for Jelco. In his haste, he failed to set forth the purpose of the corporation in the articles as required by State X laws. This defect in incorporation was so serious that Jelco was never properly formed. As such, its contract with Ted is void and no liability could attach.

Ted will counter that despite the omission, a charter was issued to Jelco by State X after the articles were filed. Jelco dealt with him as if it were a corporation. It allowed Gil to enter into contracts on its behalf, held an initial incorporator's meeting, issued stock subscriptions, and accepted Ted's services. Since Jelco dealt with Ted as if it was a valid corporation, it would operate as an injustice to allow it to deny its own validity due to a formation defect. Jelco will be estopped to deny its own existence as to its corporate obligations.

Corporation by estoppel is not a valid defense and will not relieve Jelco from its contractual liability to Ted.

2. TED v. CARL/DAN

De Jure Corporation

A de jure corporation is one organized in full or substantial compliance with the requirements of the state of incorporation.

Ted will assert that Gil prepared the articles of incorporation for Jelco. In his haste to file, he failed to set forth the purpose of the corporation. Since State X required this information, Gil's omission was not in full or substantial compliance with the mandatory State X requirements. The defect would act to void Jelco's corporate status. Carl and Dan have no corporate protection and would be held personally liable.

Jelco does not qualify as a de jure corporation.

De Facto Corporation

A de facto corporation is said to exist where there has been good faith compliance with all of the mandatory conditions precedent to incorporation under a valid statute followed by the good faith exercise of corporate powers.

Carl and Dan will contend that, although Gil failed to set forth the purpose of the corporation in the articles, it was only a result of his haste to file. This indicates that he was unaware of the defect. Despite the unintentional omission, the charter was issued to Jelco by State X after the articles were filed. The steps taken to file the articles demonstrate Gil's colorable, good faith attempt to comply with State X's valid corporate statute.

Following issuance of the charter, Gil, Carl and Dan held an initial incorporator's meeting in accordance with State X law and were duly elected as Jelco's directors. By unanimous vote, they accepted stock subscriptions and issued share certificates, all of which demonstrates their good faith exercise of corporate powers.

Ted, who would be considered a creditor, cannot question the corporate status of a de facto corporation. That function is reserved to the Secretary of State of State X.

Jelco qualifies as a de facto corporation. Carl and Dan cannot be held personally liable to Ted.

Defenses - Corporation by Estoppel

A defect in incorporation can be serious enough to deny an entity corporate existence. Nevertheless, an individual who has dealt with a corporate entity as though it was a corporation may be estopped from denying the corporate validity.

If the court does not find Jelco to be a de facto corporation, Carl and Dan will assert that when Ted contracted with Gil, the written contract stated "on behalf of Jelco, a corporation to be formed." Ted worked for Jelco for three months and looked to it for his compensation. Since he dealt with Jelco as if it were a validly formed corporation, it would operate as an injustice to allow him to later allege a defect in its formation solely for the purpose of imposing personal liability on Carl and Dan. Ted will be estopped to deny Jelco's corporate validity.

Corporation by estoppel is a valid defense and will prevent Ted from imposing personal liability on Carl and Dan.

3. ARE ART AND BOB BOUND BY THE AGREEMENT TO EACH PAY $3,000 TO JELCO?

Pre-Incorporation Stock Subscription

A pre-incorporation stock subscription is an offer of corporate stock to potential shareholders requiring acceptance and consideration.

Gil, Art and Bob met and orally agreed to each pay $3,000 for all of the Jelco stock. However, Jelco had not yet been formed. A majority of courts hold such a pre-incorporation subscription unenforceable because the corporation was not yet in existence giving it no power to contract. Thus, the agreement was merely a "continuing offer" to purchase the shares when Jelco came into existence.

When Art and Bob wrote Gil before anything further had been done stating that they "hereby revoke any agreement to subscribe to the stock of any corporation to be formed by Gil," no corporate acceptance had yet taken place. Art and Bob's revocation was valid.

In a minority of jurisdictions, Jelco would assert that A1 and Bob's agreement to buy the stock was irrevocable. Allowing Art and Bob to revoke would work hardship on Jelco. It would cause Jelco to be undercapitalized by $6,000. Gil affirmed this position by writing them that it was "impossible to rescind."

Moreover, by unanimous vote at the initial incorporator's meeting, Gil, Carl and Dan, the three Jelco directors, accepted the stock subscriptions. Although neither Art nor Bob attended that meeting, share certificates were issued to all three. Gil paid $3,000 for his shares. Such conduct would be deemed Jelco's acceptance of Art and Bob's subscription offer to become shareholders upon the formation of the corporation. As such, Art and Bob's subscriptions were binding and irrevocable at the moment the subscription was made.

Thus, Art and Bob's refusal to pay the $3,000 consideration for any stock or to participate in the business of Jelco would make them liable to Jelco and the other shareholders for any increased liability or loss which they bear as a result of the refusal. Jelco may recover the full subscription price from Art and Bob.

Depending on the jurisdiction, so will determine the validity of the stock subscription.

Defense - Effect of the State X Statute - Statute of Frauds

A contract for the sale of securities is not enforceable unless there is some writing signed by the party against whom enforcement is sought.

Art and Bob will assert that their agreement to pay $3,000 for Jelco stock was oral. The writing from Art and Bob to Gil regarding revocation did not contain the essential terms sufficient to constitute a sufficient memorandum. Absent a writing signed by Art and Bob, the contract was unenforceable.

Jelco will counter that the State X statute governed the sale of securities. The transaction in question dealt with the purchase of securities and, thus, the statute does not apply.

However, it is doubtful that the court would interpret "sale of securities" as narrowly as asserted by Jelco. Sale of securities is reasonably interpreted to mean purchase and sell. Jelco sold the securities; Bob and Art purchased them. Thus, the State X statute would govern this transaction.

Gil's letter to Art and Bob is an insufficient writing because it is not signed by either Art or Bob, the parties against whom enforcement is sought.

The State X statute will act to void the pre-incorporation stock subscription. The Statute of Frauds is a valid defense.

Estoppel

Estoppel arises when there is detrimental reliance by a promisor on the promisee's words or acts.

Jelco will argue that it needed the revenue from the stock sale to meet its financial obligations to Ted. It relied on Art and Bob's promise to buy the stock as demonstrated by its act of issuing stock certificates.

However, Art and Bob did revoke their agreement "before anything further had been done." Gil had already contracted a week earlier for Ted's services on Jelco's behalf before they entered into the oral agreement. Thus, Jelco did not detrimentally rely on the receipt of their combined $6,000 to meet any existing financial obligations.

Jelco will not prevail under an estoppel theory.

CORPORATIONS QUESTION #2

STAN v. DIXIE

The bylaws of Dixie, a publicly held corporation, provide, "The number of directors of the corporation shall be five." Insofar as pertinent, Dixie's articles of incorporation state that the number "constituting the initial board of directors" is five and provide for annual election of directors.

Since its incorporation five years ago, Dixie has been very profitable. Anticipating a hostile takeover attempt, the board voted to increase its size to nine and to stagger the terms of directors so that only three would stand for election each year.

Stan, owner of 29% of Dixie's voting stock, demanded that the board call a special meeting of shareholders to disapprove the board's action and to remove the president from office. The board refused to call a meeting for those purposes. It filled the newly created board positions with persons who were experienced in business and were close friends of the original board members. The new board entered into transactions that harmed Dixie financially but which made the corporation a less attractive target for takeover.

When Stan filed a derivative suit against Dixie and the directors challenging the board's conduct, the board appointed the new members as a "special litigation committee." Thereafter, the board moved to dismiss the suit because "based upon the recommendation of the special litigation committee, the board has concluded the suit is not in the best interests of Dixie."

1. Did the board act lawfully:

    A. In increasing its size to nine members without a shareholder vote? Discuss.

    B. In staggering the terms of board members without a shareholder vote? Discuss.

    C. In refusing to call a special meeting of shareholders? Discuss.

    D. In filling the newly created board positions without a shareholder vote? Discuss.

2. Should the court grant the board's motion to dismiss? Discuss.

Do not discuss federal securities law issues.

IRAC OUTLINE SHEET

(I)	(R)	(A)	(C)

EXAMPLE OF PROPER IRAC OUTLINE

1. DID THE BOARD ACT LAWFULLY:

A. INCREASING SIZE TO 9 MEMBERS WITHOUT A SHAREHOLDER VOTE?

(I)	(R)	(A)	(C)
AUTHORITY	Fundamental Changes Amendment Of Bylaws	The bylaws of D, a publicly held corporation, provide "The # of directors of the corp shall be 5"	Unlawful
	Amendment Of Articles	In so far as pertinent, D's articles of incorp state that the # "constituting the initial Board of Directors" is 5 Incorporation 5 years ago Anticipation a hostile takeover attempt, Board voted to increase its size to 9	
	Board Approval	Board voted to increase	
	Shareholder Approval	S owner of 29% of D's voting stock demanded the board call a special meeting of shareholders to disapprove the board's actions The board refused to call a meeting for those purposes No shareholder vote	
DEFENSE: BUSINESS JUDGMENT RULE	Good Faith/Reasonable Business Judgment	Since its incorporation 5 years ago, D has been very profitable Anticipating a hostile takeover attempt, the board voted supra The new board entered into transactions that harmed D financially but which made D a less attractive target for takeover	Invalid Defense

B. IN STAGGERING THE TERMS OF BOARD MEMBERS WITHOUT A SHAREHOLDER VOTE?

(I)	(R)	(A)	(C)
AUTHORITY	Fundamental Changes Amendment Of Articles	Articles supra & provide for annual election of directors Board voted to stagger terms of board members so that only 3 would stand for election each year	Unlawful
	Board Approval	Board voted	
	Shareholder Approval	S demanded the board call a special meeting of shareholders to disapprove supra The board refused supra	
DEFENSE: BUSINESS JUDGMENT RULE	Good Faith/Reasonable Business Judgment	Board voted to stagger Anticipating a hostile takeover	Invalid Defense

C. IN REFUSING TO CALL A SPECIAL MEETING OF SHAREHOLDERS?

(I)	(R)	(A)	(C)
SPECIAL SHAREHOLDER MEETINGS	Shareholder	S owner of 29% of D's voting stock	Lawful/Unlawful
	Proper Notice	Demanded that the board call a special meeting of shareholders	
	General Nature of Business	To disapprove the board's action (valid) To remove the president from office (invalid) The board refused in both requests	

(I)	(R)	(A)	(C)

D. IN FILLING THE NEWLY CREATED BOARD POSITIONS WITHOUT A SHREHOLDER VOTE?

AUTHORITY	Shareholder Vote	The board filled the newly created board positions w/o a shareholder vote	Lawful
DUTY OF DUE CARE	Fiduciary Duty Of Diligence/Care/Skill	It filled the newly created board positions with persons who were experienced in business The new board entered into transactions that harmed D financially	No Breach Of Duty Of Care
DEFENSE: BUSINESS JUDGMENT RULE	Good Faith/Reasonable Business Judgment	See facts under Duty of Due Care Anticipated hostile takeover supra Made D a less attractive target for takeover	Valid Defense
DUTY OF LOYALTY	Director Owes Fiduciary Duty Of Loyalty Avoid Conflicts Of Interest	It filled the newly created board positions with persons who were experienced in business & were close friends of original board members	Arguable

2. SHOULD THE COURT GRANT THE BOARD'S MOTION TO DISMISS?

DERIVATIVE SUIT	Harm To The Corporation	Board Conduct	Proper
	Demand On Directors	S demanded special meeting supra S filed a derivative suit against D & the directors challenging the board's conduct The board appointed the new members to a "special litigation committee" Thereafter, the board moved to dismiss the suit because, based upon the recommendation of the special litigation committee, the board had concluded the suit is not in the best interests of D	The Court Should Not Grant Motion
	Demand On Shareholders	Prior to filing a derivative suit S demanded that the board call a special meeting of shareholders supra The board refused	
	Contemporaneous Ownership	S owner of 29% of D's voting stock	
	Security For Costs	Post a bond?	

EXAMPLE OF IRAC CORPORATIONS ISSUE

(I) **Derivative Suit**

(R) A shareholder may bring suit on behalf of the corporation if he can establish (1) harm to the corporation, that (2) a demand on the directors and (3) the shareholders to bring suit has been made, but refused, that the shareholder was a (4) contemporaneous owner of stock at the time of the wrong and (5) he posts security for costs.

(A) Stan was unhappy with the Board's appointees. He brought suit on behalf of the corporation ostensibly to (1) prevent further harm to Dixie from the Board's improper actions.

When Stan filed a derivative suit against Dixie and its directors challenging its actions, the board appointed the new members to a "special litigation committee." Thereafter, the board moved to dismiss the suit because, "based upon the recommendation of the special litigation committee, the board had concluded the suit is not in the best interests of Dixie." This rather rapid negative response combined with the board's history of refusing Stan's previous demand for a special meeting to challenge the board's earlier actions indicates its failure to exercise reasonable care to prevent the wrong. Stan had already made sincere efforts to induce the directors to remedy wrongs with respect to increasing the board membership, staggering the terms of directors and appointing close friends to newly created positions. All his efforts had been refused. It appears that further (2) demands prior to filing his derivative suit would have been futile. Therefore, a demand on the directors will be excused.

Prior to filing his derivative suit, Stan demanded that the board call a special meeting of shareholders to disapprove of the board's actions. The board refused. Absent Stan's ability to contact other shareholders because of the board's refusal, he will be excused from making a (3) demand on the shareholders.

Stan is a 29% owner of Dixie's voting stock. His demands come on the heels of all of the directors' actions inferring that his ownership of shares was at the time of the alleged wrong. Therefore, he is a (4) contemporaneous owner. The facts are silent as to whether Stan posted a bond as (5) security for costs. Assuming that Stan did so, he has satisfied the procedural requirements to bring a derivative suit.

(C) The court should not grant the board's motion to dismiss.

SUGGESTED MODEL ANSWER

1. DID THE BOARD ACT LAWFULLY:

A. IN INCREASING ITS SIZE TO NINE MEMBERS WITHOUT A SHAREHOLDER VOTE?

Authority

Where fundamental changes in a corporation's bylaws or articles of incorporation are to be made, most jurisdictions requite both board and shareholder approval.

The bylaws of Dixie, a publicly held corporation, provide "the number of directors of the corporation shall be five." In so far as pertinent, Dixie's articles of incorporation state that the number "constituting the initial board of directors" is five. Thus, when the board acted to increase its size to nine members, it proposed a fundamental change, both in its bylaws and articles of incorporation.

The board will argue that it had been incorporated for five years. Anticipating a hostile takeover attempt, it voted for the increase. This vote was intended to thwart the hostile takeover. The articles of incorporation spoke to a five board membership only "initially" upon incorporation. Such language implies the right to increase the board's size after the "initial phase" has passed. Since the articles were intended to govern the size of the board only "initially," the board's vote approving the action after five years of incorporation was not a fundamental change.

Yet, the bylaws did not include the language "initial" as did the articles. As such, a fundamental change in the bylaws occurred with the proposed increase to nine members.

Stan, owner of 29% of Dixie's voting stock, demanded that the board call a special meeting of shareholders to disapprove of the board's action. The board refused to call a meeting for that purpose. As a result, no shareholder approval was obtained.

The board acted unlawfully by increasing its size without a shareholder vote.

Defense - Business Judgment Rule

Directors are not liable for any losses to the corporation where they exercised good faith and reasonable business judgment.

Since its incorporation five years ago, Dixie has been very profitable. Because of this profitability, and anticipating a hostile takeover attempt, the board will argue that it voted to increase its size to thwart this potential takeover attempt. Although the new board entered into transactions that financially harmed Dixie, its actions made Dixie a less attractive target for takeover. Thus, the board acted in good faith. By voting to increase its size and acting as stated, it prevented a takeover. The board's actions were an exercise of reasonable business judgment.

However, the board was acting on the mere anticipation of takeover attempt. No facts indicate that any actions had actually been taken to advance a takeover. Therefore, by voting to increase the board unilaterally without a shareholder vote, the board failed to exercise good faith and reasonable business judgment towards its shareholders.

The business judgement defense is invalid. The board acted unlawfully by increasing its size without a shareholder vote.

B. STAGGERING THE TERMS OF BOARD MEMBERS WITHOUT A SHAREHOLDER VOTE?

Authority

Defined supra.

Dixie's articles of incorporation provided for an annual election of directors. When the board voted to stagger the terms of the board members so that only three would stand for election each year, it effectively amended the articles. This action constituted a fundamental change.

The board voted far this action demonstrating its approval. Still, it did so without shareholder approval.

As discussed previously, its refusal to call a meeting pursuant to Stan's demand precluded the rights of the shareholders to approve such an action.

The shareholders can show the board's act of staggering the terms of its members would act, in effect, to freeze out minority shareholders. Any impact that the minority might have through cumulative voting rights would be eliminated because they could never unseat a quorum of directors at any one election in order to assert their rights. This is why a shareholder vote approving or disapproving the board's actions would be crucial to the rights of minority shareholders.

The board acted unlawfully by staggering the terms of the board members without a shareholder vote.

Defense - Business Judgment Rule

Defined supra.

The board will assert that, by staggering the terms of the board members, it prevented the potential for unseating a quorum of the directors. This could thwart anticipated takeover attempts. Moreover, it was the board's motivation to protect Dixie by making it a less attractive target for takeover. As such, the proposed action would be an exercise of good faith and reasonable business judgment.

However, as discussed previously, a takeover attempt was a mere anticipation at the time of the board's action. Absent more, the shareholders have a right to be involved in such decisions, particularly when minority shareholder rights can be adversely affected. The board's action was not an exercise of good faith and reasonable business judgment.

The business judgment defense is invalid. The board acted unlawfully by staggering the terms of the board members without a shareholder vote.

C. REFUSING TO CALL A SPECIAL MEETING OF SHARE- HOLDERS?

Special Shareholder Meetings

Shareholders can call special meetings if they provide proper notice of the general nature of the business to be transacted.

Stan, owner of 29% of Dixie's voting stock, demanded that the board call a special meeting of shareholders. His 29%, voting share entitled him as a Dixie shareholder to make such a demand.

If his demand was made ten days or more prior to the date of the meeting and specified the place, date and time, it would constitute proper notice.

The purpose of the special meeting was to disapprove of the board's actions previously discussed and to remove Dixie's president from office. Since shareholders have the right to approve fundamental changes in the articles of incorporation, Stan's purpose regarding disapproval of board actions was proper in relation to the general nature of Dixie's business.

However, Stan's demand was also made for purposes of removing Dixie's president from office. Removal of officers is a function reserved to the board, not the shareholders. Therefore, this purpose was not proper concerning the general nature of Dixie's business.

The directors acted lawfully by refusing to call a special meeting of the shareholders for the purpose of removing the president. However, the board acted unlawfully by refusing to call a special meeting to disapprove of the boards actions.

D. FILLING THE NEWLY CREATED BOARD POSITIONS WITH- OUT A SHAREHOLDER VOTE?

Authority

The election of board members is normally accomplished by a shareholder vote.

The board filled positions without a shareholder vote. Since shareholders generally have the right to vote for the election of directors, the board violated the shareholders rights.

However, the positions filled by the board were newly created. This necessitated the immediate appointment of members to those positions until a special or annual shareholder meeting could be scheduled where a vote could be taken.

Under these circumstances, the board acted lawfully in filling the newly created positions without a shareholder vote.

Duty of Due Care

The directors owe a fiduciary duty to the corporation and must exercise their duties with the same degree of diligence, care and skill which the ordinary prudent person would exercise in the management of his/her own affairs.

Facts state that the newly created board positions were filled with persons who were experienced in business. Because this new board entered into transactions that harmed Dixie financially, the directors may have violated their fiduciary duty to act in the best interest of Dixie. The shareholders will argue that no reasonable school of thought could justify filling director positions without a shareholder vote approving detrimental transactions. Therefore, the board members did not act with the same degree of diligence, care and skill which the ordinary prudent person would exercise in the management of his own affairs.

Nevertheless, transactions that carry a potential for profit also carry a potential for loss. These board members were experienced in business. They would know that business risks are part and parcel of any financial transaction. Therefore, absent facts that the board members acted outside the best interests of the corporation at the time they made the transaction, they will be deemed to have acted as an ordinary prudent person would have.

The board did not breach its duty of due care.

Defense - Business Judgment Rule

Defined supra.

If the court finds that the board did breach its duty of due care, the board members will argue that, by filling its newly created positions with persons who were experienced in business, even without a shareholder vote, it was seeking advice and input from persons best able to keep the Dixie corporation intact and free from an anticipated takeover attempt. Further, any financial transactions by those experienced board members were approved in good faith to prevent a threat of a hostile takeover. Mere errors in judgment that may have resulted in financial harm to Dixie are not considered below the standard of good faith. Absent facts indicating fraud or illegality, the board acted with reasonable business judgment.

The business judgment is a valid defense. The board acted properly in filling the newly created board positions without a shareholder vote.

Duty Of Loyalty

Directors owe a fiduciary duty of loyalty to promote the interests of the corporation without regard for personal gain and to avoid conflict of interest.

When the board members filled the newly created positions with persons who were their "close friends," the directors violated their fiduciary duty to Dixie. The board was furthering its own interests by bringing in cronies who would rubber stamp decisions that the current board members had already made. As such, a conflict of interest arose as the board members were promoting their own self interests rather than promoting the interests of Dixie.

The board will rebut that these new members were experienced in business. This was the main reason they were appointed. Hiring experienced business persons to run a profitable corporation that is subject to an anticipated hostile takeover attempt is crucial in order to promote the interests of that corporation. The fact that they also happened to be close friends with the board members only enhances their ability to work harmoniously and openly together. Therefore, no direct conflict existed.

Absent facts to the contrary, it appears the board may have the stronger argument.

The board may not have breached its duty of loyalty by filling the newly created board positions without a shareholder vote.

2. SHOULD THE COURT GRANT THE BOARD'S MOTION TO DISMISS?

Derivative Suit

A shareholder may bring suit on behalf of the corporation if he can establish harm to the corporation, that a demand on the directors and the shareholders to bring suit has been made, but refused, that the shareholder was a contemporaneous owner of stock at the time of the wrong and he posts security for costs.

Stan was unhappy with the Board's appointees. He brought suit on behalf of the corporation ostensibly to prevent further harm to Dixie from the Board's improper actions.

When Stan filed a derivative suit against Dixie and its directors challenging its actions, the board appointed the new members to a "special litigation committee." Thereafter, the board moved to dismiss the suit because, "based upon the recommendation of the special litigation committee, the board had concluded the suit is not in the best interests of Dixie." This rather rapid negative response combined with the board's history of refusing Stan's previous demand for a special meeting to challenge the board's earlier actions indicates its failure to exercise reasonable care to prevent the wrong. Stan had already made sincere efforts to induce the directors to remedy wrongs with respect to increasing the board membership, staggering the terms of directors and appointing close friends to newly created positions. All his efforts had been refused. It appears that further demands prior to filing his derivative suit would have been futile. Therefore, a demand on the directors will be excused.

Prior to filing his derivative suit, Stan demanded that the board call a special meeting of shareholders to disapprove of the board's actions. The board refused. Absent Stan's ability to contact other shareholders because of the board's refusal, he will be excused from making a demand on the shareholders.

Stan is a 29% owner of Dixie's voting stock. His demands come on the heels of all of the directors' actions inferring that his ownership of shares was at the time of the alleged wrong. Therefore, he is a contemporaneous owner.

The facts are silent as to whether Stan posted a bond as security for costs. Assuming that Stan did so, he has satisfied the procedural requirements to bring a derivative suit.

The court should not grant the board's motion to dismiss.

CORPORATIONS QUESTION #3

SOL v. CHARE

In 1972, Ida bought 50,000 shares of Martco. In 1975, Martco contracted with Buildco for the construction of four new stores for $4 million. At the Martco board meeting at which the Buildco contract was to be considered, Chare, Martco's chairman, revealed that he had been a director of Buildco since 1972 but that he had not participated as a member of the Buildco board in approving this contract. Chare, believing it to be a fair contract, joined the other four Martco directors in voting to approve the contract. In fact, subsequent investigation revealed that the price charged by Buildco under the contract was excessive and unfair to Martco.

In 1976, Ida died, leaving her stock to her son Sol. Unhappy about Chare's leadership, Sol asked Chare for Martco's shareholder list to solicit proxies to unseat Chare at the 1978 annual meeting. Chare, fearing Sol's success, refused, and Sol was unable to gain a seat on the board. Later Sol learned that Waters, another shareholder, would have given Sol his proxy. Between the two, they owned sufficient shares to elect one director under Martco's cumulative voting rule.

At the September 30, 1978 director's meeting, Chare announced that Martco had suffered a $10 million loss during the last fiscal year and that this information would be released to the public on October 15. He tendered his resignation, which was accepted effective immediately.

Between October 5 and October 10, Chare sold 100,000 shares of Martco stock, his entire holdings, for $25 per share, the current market price. After the loss announcement on October 15, Martco stock dropped to $10 per share. Sol asked the remaining directors to bring suit against Chare but they refused.

Assume no federal security laws are applicable.

1) What, if any, is Chare's personal liability to Sol? Discuss.

2) Assuming Sol brings a shareholder's derivative action against Chare, what is the probable success of such suit in connection with each of the above transactions? Discuss.

IRAC OUTLINE SHEET

(I)	(R)	(A)	(C)

EXAMPLE OF PROPER IRAC OUTLINE

1. SOL (S) v. CHARE (C) - PERSONAL LIABILITY

(I)	(R)	(A)	(C)
COMMON LAW: INSPECTION OF CORPORATE RECORDS	Shareholder 's Right To Inspect	1972 Ida bought 50,000 shares 1976 Ida died leaving her stock to son S	Violation Of Right
	Reasonable Time	At 1978 annual meeting	
	Proper Purpose	Unhappy about C's leadership, S asked C for M's shareholder list to solicit proxies to unseat C C fearing S's success, refused	
INSPECTION OF SHAREHOLDER LIST	Shareholder Right To Inspect Shareholder Lists	1976 Ida left stock to S S asked C for M's shareholder list	Violation Of Right
	Proper Purpose	Solicit proxies to unseat C supra C, fearing S's success, refused S unable to gain seat on board S later learned that W, a shareholder, would have given S his proxy Between S &W, owned sufficient shares to elect one director under cumulative voting rule	

2. SOL (S) v. CHARE (C) - DERIVATIVE ACTION:

(I)	(R)	(A)	(C)
DERIVATIVE SUIT	Harm To The Corporation	Unhappy about leadership of M	Proper
	Demand On The Directors	S asked remaining directors to bring suit against C/they refused	
	Demand On Shareholder	S asked for shareholder list/C refused	
	Contemporaneous Ownership	1972 Ida bought shares supra In 1975 B contract In 1976 Ida died leaving stock to S (operation of law)	
	Security For Costs	Post a bond?	

C'S APPROVAL OF THE MARTCO (M) /BUILDCO (B) CONTRACT:

(I)	(R)	(A)	(C)
DUTY OF LOYALTY INTERLOCKING DIRECTORATES	Director Owes Fiduciary Duty Of Loyalty - Interlocking Directorates	C M's chairman & a director of B at the time of the B/M contract for construction of four new stores for $4 million	Breach Of Duty Of Loyalty
	Full Disclosure	At M board meeting, C revealed he'd been a director of B since 1972 but had not participated as a member of B board in approval of B/M contract	
	Disinterested Majority Ratification	C joined the other four M directors in voting to approve the contract	
	Fair Transaction	C believed it to be a fair contract Subsequent investigation revealed that price charged was excessive & unfair to M	
DUTY OF CARE	Fiduciary Duty Of Diligence/Care/Skill	Subsequent investigation revealed price excessive supra C believed B contract fair	Breach Of Duty Of Care
DEFENSE: BUSINESS JUDGMENT RULE	Good Faith/Reasonable Business Judgment	C believed contract fair Subsequent investigation supra	Invalid Defense

C'S SALE OF 100,000 SHARES OF MARTCO STOCK:

(I)	(R)	(A)	(C)
COMMON LAW: DUTY TO SHAREHOLDERS	Insider/Director/Officer	C, M's past chairman (insider?)	No Duty Owed
	No Duty To Disclose To Shareholders	S, M shareholder M suffered $10 million loss during last fiscal year & info would be released to public on 10/15	

(I)	(R)	(A)	(C)
EXCEPTION: SPECIAL FACTS DOCTRINE	Insider/Director/Officer	C chairman of M C tendered resignation/accepted immediately (insider?)	No Special Facts No Duty Owed
	Trades On The Basis Of Special Information	At 9/30/78 meeting, C had inside information, not yet public, that M had suffered a $10 million loss	
	Failed To Disclose The Information	Between 10/5 & 10/10 C sold 100,000 shares at $25 per After announcement on 10/15/78, shares dropped to $10/share Loss $15/share	
	Privity Existed	S a M shareholder / Seller?	
COMMON LAW: DUTY TO CORPORATION	Fiduciary Duty To Disclose Inside Information	C, M past chairman M $10 million loss not public until 10/15 supra	Duty Owed
	Corporate Asset	M shares	
	Disgorge Profits	Between 10/5-10/10 C sold for $25/share supra After release of information, stock dropped to $10/share supra Profit $15/share = $1,500,000	

EXAMPLE OF IRAC CORPORATIONS OUTLINE

(I) **Duty of Loyalty - Interlocking Directorate**

(R) Directors owe a fiduciary duty of loyalty to promote the interests of the corporation without regard for personal gain. Interlocking directorates may constitute a conflict of interest unless the director makes (1) a full disclosure of the interest to the other directors, (2) the disinterested majority of directors ratify the interest and (3) the transaction is fair.

(A) Sol will allege that Chare was both the chairman of the board of Martco and a member of the board of directors of Buildco at the time Martco voted to award Buildco a contract to construct four new stores for $4 million. Chare would owe a fiduciary duty to both Martco and Buildco. Thus, Chare's position on both boards simultaneously constituted interlocking directorates which resulted in a conflict of interest.

Chare will rebut that at the Martco board meeting, he revealed to the other directors that he had been a director of Buildco since 1972 but had not participated as a member of the Buildco board in the approval of the Martco/Buildco contract. His (1) full disclosure of these facts was made to the remaining Martco directors before they voted.

While Chare joined with the remaining directors in voting to approve the Buildco contract, the four remaining directors had no personal interest in the transaction. Although Chare's vote would not be counted under common law, the four remaining directors who voted to ratify the transaction would constitute (2) a disinterested majority of the total five directors sufficient for a quorum.

However, Sol will establish that despite Chare's belief that the contract was fair subsequent investigation revealed that the contract price was excessive and (3) unfair to Martco. At common law, such a contract was void from its inception. At modern law, the contract is voidable since it was discovered to be unfair. Chare has the burden of proof if he seeks to rebut the presumption of unfairness.

(C) Therefore, it appears that Chare breached her duty of loyalty to Martco.

SUGGESTED MODEL ANSWER

SOL v. CHARE

1) PERSONAL LIABILITY TO SOL:

Common Law - Inspection of Corporate Records

At common law, a shareholder has a right to inspect corporate records at reasonable times provided that the shareholder proves a proper purpose.

In 1972, Ida bought 50,000 shares of Martco Stock. In 1976, she died leaving her 50,000 shares of Martco stock to her son, Sol. This bequest gave rise to Sol's right as a shareholder.

Unhappy about Chare's leadership, Sol asked Chare for the shareholder list in order to solicit proxies for the purpose of unseating Chare. Sol's request to inspect Martco's shareholder list at the annual meeting would be proper provided a reasonable time was selected. Sol is seeking inspection to protect his interest as a shareholder, which is a proper purpose.

Chare refused to permit Sol's inspection of these corporate records because he feared Sol's success in unseating him. Chare's refusal, on this basis, is improper.

Sol's common law right to inspect corporate records was violated.

Inspection of Shareholder Lists

A shareholder has a right to inspect shareholders lists provided the shareholder proves a proper purpose.

In 1976, Ida left Martco stock to Sol when she died. Thus, at the time Sol asked Chare for the shareholder list, he was a shareholder of 50,000 shares of Martco stock. He had the right to inspect the shareholder list to "solicit proxies to unseat Chare." Since proxy solicitation is reasonably related to the interest of the shareholder, Sol has alleged a proper purpose. Sol had a right to inspect the list.

Chare's reason for refusing Sol's request was motivated by his fear that Sol would succeed in unseating him. Therefore, the management refusal was made for an improper purpose. In addition, it was only because of Chare' s refusal that Sol was unable to gain a seat on the Board. Waters, another shareholder, would have given Sol his proxy. Between Sol and Waters, there were a sufficient number of shares to elect Sol under Martco's cumulative voting rules.

Sol will be entitled to an injunction invalidating the 1978 vote and authorizing a new vote. Sol will also be given access to the shareholder list for the purpose of soliciting proxies.

However, Chare will incur no personal liability to Sol.

2) PROBABLE SUCCESS OF DERIVATIVE ACTION IN CONNECTION WITH EACH TRANSACTION:

Derivative Suit

A shareholder may bring suit on behalf of the corporation if he can establish harm to the corporation, that a demand on the directors and the shareholders to bring suit has been made but refused, that the shareholder was a contemporaneous owner of stock at the time of the wrong and he posts security for costs.

Sol was unhappy with Martco's leadership. He brought suit on the behalf of the corporation, ostensibly to prevent further harm to it from ineffective leadership.

Sol asked the remaining directors of Martco to bring suit against Chare but they refused. Therefore, any further demand would be futile.

The facts do not indicate whether Sol made a demand on the shareholders. Sol will argue that he had no access to the shareholder list because of Chare's refusal. Therefore, he was unable to make a demand. As a general rule, a demand on the shareholders is not required in a public corporation. Therefore, Sol may be excused of the requirement to make a demand on the shareholders.

However, Chare will argue that the Buildco contract was made in 1975. Sol did not obtain his stock until 1976. Since Sol was not an owner at the time of the alleged wrong, Sol did not meet the requirement of contemporaneous ownership.

Sol will counter that an exception to the contemporaneous ownership rule applies when the shareholder received his shares by operation of law. Ida bought her shares in 1972. The Buildco contract was made in 1975. Sol inherited his shares from Ida in 1976. Thus, Sol would be considered a holder of the shares by operation of law at the time of the wrong.

The facts are silent as to whether Sol posted a bond as security for costs. Assuming that Sol did so, he has met all of the prerequisites necessary to bring a derivative suit.

Therefore, it appears a derivative suit is proper.

CHARE'S APPROVAL OF THE MARTCO/BUILDCO CONTRACT

Duty of Loyalty - Interlocking Directorate

Directors owe a fiduciary duty of loyalty to promote the interests of the corporation without regard for personal gain. Interlocking directorates may constitute a conflict of interest unless the director makes a full disclosure of the interest to the other directors, the disinterested majority of directors ratify the interest and the transaction is fair.

Chare was both the chairman of the board of Martco and a member of the board of directors of Buildco at the time Martco voted to award Buildco a contract to construct four new stores for $4 million. Chare would owe a fiduciary duty to both Martco and Buildco. Thus, Chare's position on both boards simultaneously constituted interlocking directorates which resulted in a conflict of interest.

Chare will rebut that at the Martco board meeting, he revealed to the other directors that he had been a director of Buildco since 1972 but had not participated as a member of the Buildco board in the approval of the Martco/Buildco contract. His full disclosure of these facts was made to the remaining Martco directors before they voted.

While Chare joined with the remaining directors in voting to approve the Buildco contract, the four remaining directors had no personal interest in the transaction. Although Chare's vote would not be counted under common law, the four remaining directors who voted to ratify the transaction would constitute a disinterested majority of the total five directors sufficient for a quorum.

However, Sol will establish that despite Chare's belief that the contract was fair, subsequent investigation revealed that the contract price was excessive and unfair to Martco. At common law, such a contract was void from its inception. At modern law, the contract is voidable since it was discovered to be unfair. Chare has the burden of proof if he seeks to rebut the presumption of unfairness.

Therefore, it appears that Chare breached her duty of loyalty to Martco.

Duty of Care

Directors owe a fiduciary duty to the corporation and must exercise their duties with the same degree of diligence, care and skill that the ordinary prudent person would exercise in the management of his/her own affairs.

Sol will contend that Chare's and the other directors' vote to approve the Martco/Buildco contract was premature. Because all the directors owed a fiduciary duty to Martco, they should have investigated before approving the contract. By failing to discover unfairness that was ultimately revealed by a subsequent investigation, they failed to exercise the diligence, care and skill which an ordinary prudent person would exercise in the management of his own affairs.

Chare and the directors believed the Buildco contract was fair. Only upon a subsequent investigation was it revealed that the contract price was unfair and excessive. Thus, at the time they voted to approve the contract, the directors acted on a belief of fairness indicating proper prudence.

Still, the directors failure to properly investigate would equate to a lack of due diligence, care and skill.

Therefore, the directors breached their duty of care.

Defense - Business Judgment Rule

Directors are not liable for any losses to the corporation where they exercised good faith and reasonable business judgment.

Chare will assert that he and the other directors voted to approve the contract because they thought it was fair. Their approval of the contract was made on this good faith belief.

Despite the subsequent investigation which ultimately revealed an excessive contract price, the directors are not responsible for these losses to Martco that resulted from an exercise of reasonable business judgment.

However, had the investigation been conducted prior to the vote to contract, the excessive price could have been avoided. Failure to make reasonable efforts to obtain sufficient facts upon which to make a decision under the circumstances amounts to a lack of good faith. The directors failure to do so indicates lack of reasonable judgment in the decision making process.

Therefore, the business judgment rule will not protect Chare from liability.

CHARE'S SALE OF 100,000 SHARES OF MARTCO STOCK

Common Law Duty to Shareholders

At common law, corporate insiders, directors and officers owed no duty to disclose information to the shareholder prior to sale unless special facts known only by the insider would have caused the shareholder to act differently.

Chare, as Martco's past chairman, is an insider. Sol is a Martco shareholder. At common law, Chare would have no duty to disclose to Sol the nonpublic information concerning Martco's $10 million loss absent special facts.

Special Facts Doctrine

An insider, director or officer who trades on the basis of special information and fails to disclose that information will be liable to shareholders in privity with him.

Chare was Martco's chairman at the time that he learned that Martco has suffered a $10 million loss. Chare tendered his resignation as chairman on September 30, 1978. It was accepted as effective immediately. His status is that of an insider.

At the September 30, 1978 directors' meeting, he made the announcement stating that this information would be released to the public on October 15, 1978. His subsequent sale of his 100,000 Martco shares between October 5 - October 10, 1978 for $25 per share was a result of special information he has obtained as a result of his status as an ex-chairman. If so, it would be deemed inside information.

Chare had a duty to disclose the information to the buyer shareholders prior to the trade. The facts indicate that after the loss announcement became public, Martco stock dropped to $10 per share. Thus, as a result of his failure to disclose, the injured buyers lost $15 per share.

However, Chare will successfully establish that the common law extended a duty to disclose only to the injured Seller directly involved in the trades. Sol was a Martco shareholder but not an injured Seller. No privity existed between Chare and Sol.

Therefore, Sol may not bring suit against Chare under the common law special fact doctrine.

Common Law Duty to the Corporation

Pursuant to the court's ruling in Diamond v. Oreamuno, an insider owes a common law fiduciary duty to the corporation to disclose inside information prior to the sale of stock because such information is considered a corporate asset. Failure to do so will result in the disgorging of the profits.

As the past chairman of the Martco board, Chare was an insider. He owed a fiduciary duty to Martco to disclose the information about the $10 million loss he acquired prior to the public announcement to the buyer shareholders to whom he was making the sale.

Chare failed to disclose the information to the buyers prior to his trades. He did not advise Martco of his sales activity resulting from this inside information. Therefore, Chare took advantage of a corporate asset.

Chare's stock was selling for $25 per share at the time of the trades. After the release of the information regarding the loss, the corporate shares were selling for $10 per share. Chare made a profit of $15 per share totaling $1,500,000. The <u>profits</u> from the sales will be <u>disgorged</u> and paid to Martco.

Therefore, the $1,500,000 will be ordered paid to Martco by way of Sol's derivative suit.

CORPORATIONS QUESTION #4

AJAX v. BABB

Ajax Mfg. Corp. has issued 250,000 shares of $50 par value common stock. 10,000 of such shares were reacquired and are currently held as treasury stock. After a board meeting in which possible Ajax plant expansion sites were discussed, Babb, one of Ajax's nine directors, paid $3,000 to obtain an option to purchase one of those sites, at a purchase price of $120,000. Ajax had allocated $250,000 for site acquisition. When the other directors later learned that Babb had acquired the option, they demanded that he assign it to the corporation for the option price of $3,000.

At a subsequent board meeting, the directors voted to purchase Whiteacre for $50,000 from Carl, a director, who had acquired it for $10,000 before becoming a director.

The board also voted to sell the 10,000 treasury shares for $71 per share to Dale, who had been offered employment by Ajax as Vice President-Finance. Dale insisted on becoming a shareholder as a condition to accepting the offered employment, and agreed to the price of the stock. Earl, an Ajax shareholder, seeks to enjoin this sale, claiming that it violates his preemptive rights.

At the same meeting, the board approved the sale of Greenacre for $50,000. It had been purchased by Ajax five years ago for $70,000.

Fox, Vice President-Operations for Ajax, heard that Gert, an Ajax shareholder, was annoyed with management and was offering to sell her shares for $65 each. The latest financial report for Ajax, distributed to all shareholders, indicated that Ajax stock had a book value of $70.50. Fox purchased Gert's shares at her price.

Discuss the following:

(a) The demand that Babb assign his option to purchase the expansion site to Ajax;

(b) The propriety of Ajax's purchase of Whiteacre from Carl for $50,000;

(c) Earl's right to enjoin the sale of 10,000 shares of treasury stock to Dale;

(d) The propriety of the sale of Greenacre for $50,000;

(e) Fox's liability, if any, by reason of his purchase of Gert's shares.

IRAC OUTLINE SHEET

(I)	(R)	(A)	(C)

EXAMPLE OF PROPER IRAC OUTLINE

AJAX v. BABB

(a) AJAX'S (A) DEMAND THAT BABB (B) ASSIGN HIS OPTION TO PURCHASE EXPANSION SITE

(I)	(R)	(A)	(C)
DUTY OF LOYALTY CORPORATE OPPORTUNITY DOCTRINE	Director Owes Fiduciary Duty Of Loyalty	B one of A's nine directors	Breach Of Duty Of Loyalty
	Bars Usurpation Of Legitimate Corporate Opportunity	After board meeting in which possible plant expansion sites discussed, B paid $3,000 to obtain an option to purchase one of those sites at a purchase price of $120,000 A had allocated $250,000 for site acquisition When other directors learned that B had acquired option, they demanded assignment to A for option price of $3,000 Assignment of option to A or constructive trust	

(b) AJAX'S (A) PURCHASE OF WHITEACRE FROM CARL (C) FOR $50,000

(I)	(R)	(A)	(C)
DUTY OF CARE	Fiduciary Duty of Diligence/Care/Skill	Expansion sites discussed supra At a subsequent board meeting, directors voted to purchase Whiteacre for $50,000 from C, a director who has acquired it for $10,000 before becoming a director	No Breach Of Duty
DEFENSE: BUSINESS JUDGMENT RULE	Good Faith/Reasonable Business Judgment	C purchased Whiteacre for $10,000 before becoming a director Directors voted to purchase for $50,000 supra	Valid Defense
DUTY OF LOYALTY INTERESTED DIRECTOR TRANSACTION	Director Owes Fiduciary Duty Of Loyalty - Interested Director	Directors voted to purchase Whiteacre for $50,000 from C supra who had acquired it for $10,000 before becoming a director	No Breach Of Duty Of Loyalty
	Full Disclosure	Directors voted to purchase Whiteacre from C for $50,000	
	Disinterested Majority Ratification	A's nine directors voted to purchase	
	Fair Transaction	Directors voted to purchase for $50,000 C acquired for $10,000	

(c) EARL'S (E) RIGHT TO ENJOIN SALE OF 10,000 SHARES OF TREASURY STOCK TO DALE (D)

(I)	(R)	(A)	(C)
PREEMPTIVE RIGHTS	Common Law/Modern Law	Ajax articles/bylaws?	No Preemptive Rights
	Existing Shareholder	E, an Ajax shareholder	
	Proportionate Interest In Newly Issued Stock	250,00 shares common stock issued 10,000 share reacquired & currently held as treasury stock	
	Issued For Cash	Board voted to sell 10,000 shares of treasury stock to D for $71.00 per share Earl seeks to enjoin sale	
DUTY OF CARE	Fiduciary Duty Of Diligence/Care/Skill	Board voted to sell 10,000 shares of treasury stock for $71/share to D who had been offered employment by A as VP D insisted on becoming a shareholder as a condition to accepting the offered employ & agreed to the price Book value $70.50 per share	No Breach Of Care

(I)	(R)	(A)	(C)
DEFENSE: BUSINESS JUDGMENT RULE	Good Faith/Reasonable Business Judgment	D agreed to $71/share supra Book value was $70.50/share supra Condition of employment	Valid Defense

(d) SALE OF GREENACRE FOR $50,000

(I)	(R)	(A)	(C)
DUTY OF CARE	Fiduciary Duty Of Diligence/Care/Skill	At same meeting, board approved a sale of Greenacre for $50,000 It had been purchased by Ajax 5 years before for $70,000	Arguable
DEFENSE: BUSINESS JUDGMENT RULE	Good Faith/Reasonable Business Judgment	Sale $50,000/purchased for $70,000 supra	Arguable

(e) FOX'S (F) LIABILITY FOR THE PURCHASE OF GERT'S (G) SHARES

(I)	(R)	(A)	(C)
INSIDER TRADING-10b55	Interstate Commerce Fraud Or Manipulation Connection With Purchase Or Sale Of Securities	F heard G was offering to sell F purchased G's shares (instrumentality?)	No Jurisdiction
COMMON LAW: DUTY TO SHAREHOLDERS	Insider/Director/Officer No Duty To Disclose To Shareholders	F Vice President G a shareholder of A Book value $70.50/share	No Duty Owed
EXCEPTION: SPECIAL FACTS DOCTRINE	Insider/Director/Officer	F Vice President	No Special Facts No Duty Owed
	Trades On The Basis Of Special Information	Heard that G was unhappy with management/was offering to sell her shares at $65.00	
	Failed To Disclose Information	Latest financial reports distributed to all shareholders indicated stock value of $70.50	
	Privity Existed	F purchased G's shares at her price	
COMMON LAW: DUTY TO CORPORATION	Fiduciary Duty To Disclose Inside Information	F Vice President of A Heard G offering to sell for $65/share Information distributed supra	Duty Owed
	Corporate Asset	A shares	
	Disgorge Profits	Value $70.50 Purchase $65.00 Profit $5.50 per share	

EXAMPLE OF IRAC CORPORATIONS ISSUE

(I) **Preemptive Rights**

(R) At common law, the articles of incorporation and bylaws assured (1) existing shareholders (2) a proportionate interest in any (3) newly authorized shares issued for cash. Modernly, existing shareholders are not guaranteed protection of their proportionate share of the corporation.

(A) The facts are silent as to whether the Ajax articles of incorporation or bylaws are of the common law or modern law type.

Assuming the common law applies, Earl will argue that he is (1) an existing Ajax shareholder. 250,000 shares of Ajax common stock were initially issued. The board sold 10,000 shares of treasury stock to Dale for $71.00 per share as a condition to his accepting a position as vice president of the corporation. Earl will argue that his (2) proportionate interest in the company's 250,000 shares of issued stock was altered as a result.

However, the board will argue that the shares sold to Dale were reacquired shares held as treasury stock. While the shares were sold to Dale for $71.00 and, therefore, issued for cash, they were not (3) newly issued stock.

(C) Thus, no preemptive rights attach and Earl cannot enjoin the sale.

SUGGESTED MODEL ANSWER

(A) AJAX'S DEMAND THAT BABB ASSIGN HIS OPTION TO PURCHASE EXPANSION SITE:

Duty of Loyalty - Corporate Opportunity Doctrine

Directors owes a fiduciary duty of loyalty to promote the interests of the corporation without regard for personal gain. The duty includes barring any director of the corporation from usurping any legitimate corporate opportunities of the corporation.

Babb was one of Ajax's nine corporate directors. As such, he owned Ajax a fiduciary duty of loyalty to act in the best interests of the corporation without regard for personal gain.

The facts indicate that during a corporate meeting, several possible plant expansion sites were discussed. Since the corporation had a present interest in these properties and was actively considering them for a specific expansion need, these sites were legitimate corporate opportunities.

After the board meeting, Babb paid $3,000 to obtain an option to purchase one of the sites discussed at the meeting at a purchase price of $120,000. He did so knowing that Ajax was interested in the site. Ajax had allocated $250,000 for property acquisition. This allocation demonstrates its ability to afford the site. Because Babb failed to fully disclose and give Ajax the right to reject the site before he purchased it, he usurped a legitimate corporate opportunity.

Babb's conduct indicates that he acted in his own best interests rather than in the interests of Ajax.

When the other Ajax directors learned that Babb had acquired the option, they demanded that Babb assign the option to Ajax for the option price of $3,000. They may compel him to do so through a forced assignment or a constructive trust remedy.

Babb breached his duty of loyalty to Ajax.

(B) AJAX'S PURCHASE OF WHITEACRE FROM CARL FOR $50,000:

Duty of Care

Directors owe a fiduciary duty to the corporation and must exercise their duties with the same degree of diligence, care and skill that the ordinary prudent person would exercise in the management of his/her own affairs.

The Ajax directors voted to purchase Whiteacre from Carl, a fellow corporate director for $50,000. Thus, a fiduciary duty was owed to Ajax regarding this transaction. Carl had purchased Whiteacre for $10,000 before becoming an Ajax director. Since the directors voted to pay him a price that resulted in a $40,000 profit, this could be seen as a failure to exercise diligence, care and skill in negotiating a purchase price.

However, although Carl owned the property prior to becoming a director, there are no facts to suggest that he intended to take advantage of the corporation through the sale of the property. If Whiteacre was worth $50,000 at the time of the purchase vote, the directors' decision to purchase it at that price was a proper exercise of care and skill. Ajax was looking for expansion sites when the directors voted to purchase it. Assuming it was an appropriate site, they were acting as ordinary and prudent persons exercising the same skills as if managing their own affairs.

The directors did not breach their duty of care.

Defense - Business Judgment Rule

Directors are not liable for any losses to the corporation where they exercised good faith and reasonable business judgment.

Carl initially purchased Whiteacre for $10,000 before becoming a director. The directors will argue that there are no facts to indicate that the $50,000 purchase price that they voted to pay was in excess of its true value at the time of its purchase by Ajax. Therefore, they acted in good faith. Since land normally appreciates in value, it may be argued that the value of Whiteacre had appreciated to $50,000 or more at the time of the Ajax acquisition. Thus, the purchase was an exercise of reasonable business judgment.

It is Ajax's burden of proof to show losses to the corporation or that the directors did not exercise good faith and reasonable business judgment. Absent any further facts, it is unlikely that any Ajax shareholder could meet its burden of proof.

It appears that the business judgment defense will apply.

Duty of Loyalty - Interested Director

Directors owe a fiduciary duty of loyalty to promote the interests of the corporation without regard for personal gain. Where an interested director is involved in a transaction with the corporation, he must make full disclosure to and obtain ratification from a disinterested majority of the directors. The court will look to the fairness of the transaction to determine whether there has been a breach of the duty of loyalty.

The directors voted to purchase Whiteacre for $50,000 from Carl who had acquired it for $10,000 before becoming a director. This resulted in a $40,000 personal gain to Carl. Such a significant financial interest could be interpreted as self-dealing violating Carl's fiduciary duty of loyalty to act in the best interests of Ajax without regard for personal gain.

However, the facts do not indicate that Carl, an interested director, failed to inform the other directors of his ownership or of its original purchase price. Absent facts to the contrary, it may be assumed that the directors first obtained a full disclosure of all relevant information concerning the value of the property and its ownership before they voted on its acquisition.

The facts state that Ajax had nine directors who voted to purchase Whiteacre. As an interested director, Carl's vote on the sale would not be counted. However, the votes of the eight remaining directors who had no personal interest in the property would be counted as a quorum. Therefore, such ratification was by a disinterested majority.

Finally, as established previously, there are no facts indicating that the purchase price was unfair or excessive. Thus, the transaction appears fair.

The directors did not violate their duty of loyalty to Ajax.

(C) EARL'S RIGHT TO ENJOIN SALE OF TREASURY STOCK TO DALE:

Preemptive Rights

At common law, the articles of incorporation and bylaws assured existing shareholders a proportionate interest in any newly authorized shares issued for cash. Modernly, existing shareholders are not guaranteed protection of their proportionate share of the corporation.

The facts are silent as to whether the Ajax articles of incorporation or bylaws are of the common law or modern law type.

Assuming the common law applies, Earl will argue that he is an existing Ajax shareholder. 250,000 shares of Ajax common stock were initially issued. The board sold 10,000 shares of treasury stock to Dale for $71.00 per share as a condition to his accepting a position as vice president of the corporation. His proportionate interest in the company's 250,000 shares of issued stock was altered as a result.

Yet, the shares sold to Dale were reacquired shares held as treasury stock. While the shares were sold to Dale for $71.00 and, therefore, issued for cash, they were not newly issued stock.

Thus, no preemptive rights attach and Earl cannot enjoin the sale.

Duty of Care

Defined supra.

Earl will contend the board voted to sell 10,000 shares to Dale for $71.00 per share. It was improperly using the treasury stock to entice Dale to accept a position as vice president. Earl will assert that this action equated to a breach of the board's fiduciary duty to Ajax. As such, the directors did not act with the diligence, care and skill of a ordinary prudent person in the management of his own affairs.

However, Dale insisted on becoming a shareholder as a condition to accepting the offered employ and he agreed to the price. Ajax's agreement to sell him treasury shares as part of his employment was an exercise of reasonable prudence for the purpose of securing a qualified vice president. Further, the stock was sold to Dale at $71.00 per share. This was 50 cents above the book value of $70.50 per share. Thus, the sale was an exercise of proper care, skill and judgment in the management of corporate affairs.

Therefore, the sale was not a breach of the duty of care.

Defense - Business Judgment Rule

Defined supra.

The directors will argue that Dale paid $71.00 per share for shares that had a book value of $70.50. The sale reaped a 50 cent per share profit for the corporation. In addition, the sale secured Dale's employment. This clearly demonstrates their good faith dealing. Furthermore, the shares did not represent an improper payment of salary for future services. It was merely a condition of employment. It appears that the directors demonstrated reasonable business judgment by securing a qualified vice president while at the same time earning money for the corporation.

Proper business judgment will shield the directors from any liability.

(D) SALE OF GREENACRE FOR $50,000:

Duty of Care

Defined supra.

At the same board meeting previously discussed, the board approved the sale of Greenacre for $50,000. It had been purchased five years before for $70,000. Such a sale would result in a

$20,000 loss to the corporation. A breach of the board's fiduciary duty to Ajax may have occurred. Given the fact that land normally appreciates in value, it may be argued that such a loss to the corporation indicates that the board was not acting with the degree of diligence, care and skill expected of a ordinary prudent person in the management of his own affairs.

Therefore, the sale may have been a breach of the duty of care.

Defense - Business Judgment Rule

Defined supra.

At the time of the purchase of Greenacre, the property was worth $70,000. If the property depreciated in value to $50,000 over the course of five years through no fault of the board, selling it before it incurred further losses would demonstrate that the directors were acting in good faith. Absent facts to show that the property could have been sold for more money, the directors exercised reasonable business judgment.

The burden of proof is on the plaintiff to show a breach of the duty of care. Absent a showing of bad faith by the board, it is unlikely that a complaining shareholder could establish a breach of the business judgment rule.

It appears that the business judgment rule may be a valid defense.

(E) FOX'S LIABILITY FOR THE PURCHASE OF GERT'S SHARES:

Insider Trading - l0b-5

SEC Rule 10b-5 states that it is unlawful for any person, directly or indirectly, by use of any means or instrumentality of interstate commerce or the mails, to employ any fraudulent or manipulative devices in connection with the purchase or sale of securities.

The facts stated that Fox heard Gert was offering to sell her shares for $65.00 each. There is no indication that Fox used an instrumentality of interstate commerce to accomplish the purchase of Gert's shares.

Thus, in the absence of the necessary jurisdiction, there has been no l0b-5 violation.

Common Law Duty to Shareholders

At common law, corporate insiders, directors and officers owed no duty to disclose information to the shareholder prior to sale unless special facts known only by the insider would have caused the shareholder to act differently.

As a Vice President of Ajax, Fox was an officer of the corporation. Gert was an Ajax shareholder. At common law, Fox would have no duty to disclose to Gert that the true value of the stock was $70.50 absent special facts.

Special Facts Doctrine

An insider, director or officer who trades on the basis of special information and fails to disclose that information will be liable to shareholders in privity with him.

Fox was vice president of operations. Because of his position as an Ajax officer, he had special information that the value of Gert's shares was greater than the $65.00 per share she was offering for sale of her shares.

Nonetheless, Fox had simply "heard" that Gert was unhappy and wanted to sell her shares for $65.00. The latest financial reports distributed to all shareholders, including Gert, indicated the stock's value at $70.50 per share. Gert should have known the value of her shares at the time of the sale since the information was readily available. Thus, the purchase of Gert's shares at $65.00 was not due to Fox's failure to disclose special facts known only to him.

It appears that Fox did not breach his common law duty to Gert under the special facts doctrine.

Common Law Duty to the Corporation

Pursuant to the court's ruling in Diamond v. Oreamuno, an insider owes a common law fiduciary duty to the corporation to disclose inside information prior to the sale of stock because such information is considered a corporate asset. Failure to do so will result in the disgorging of the profits.

As an Ajax vice president, Fox was an insider. When he heard that Gert was unhappy with management and was willing to sell her shares for $65.00 each, he owed a fiduciary duty to Ajax to disclose Gert's willingness to sell her shares for less than their $70.50 book value. If he had done so, Ajax would have taken advantage of its right to purchase the shares from Gert.

Fox would rebut that since he heard about Gert's willingness to sell, the information was also readily accessible to Ajax as well. If so, he had no duty to disclose.

However, when Fox purchased the Ajax stock for himself without first disclosing his intentions, he profited by unlawfully converting a corporate asset.

If the corporation can successfully show that Fox breached his fiduciary duty to the corporation, it will recover the difference between the $70.50 book value of the stock and the $65.00 sale price paid by Fox. The profits of $5.50 per share will be disgorged and paid to Ajax.

Therefore, Ajax can recover against Fox.

CORPORATIONS QUESTION #5

TCO v. ACO

Acquirer, Inc. (ACO) and Target, Inc. (TCO) are corporations. All sales and purchases described below were conducted through a national stock exchange.

On December 1, 1986, ACO bought 120,000 TCO shares for $5 per share, thereby becoming a 12% TCO shareholder. ACO never previously owned any TCO stock. ACO immediately notified TCO's chief executive officer, Dan, that it had made the purchase and that it was considering a tender offer for the rest of TCO's stock at $9 per share.

The next day, Dan's personal lawyer, Len, warned Dan not to buy TCO stock until ACO's stock purchase and acquisition plans became public. On the same day, Dan told his son, Sam, about the proposed acquisition. On December 3, 1986, Len and Sam each bought 10,000 TCO shares for $5 per share.

On December 4, 1986, ACO filed appropriate disclosure documents with the Securities and Exchange Commission (SEC), and ACO and TCO separately issued press releases about the stock purchase and the proposed acquisition.

On December 5, 1986, Len and Sam each sold their 10,000 TCO shares for $8.50 per share. ACO sold its TCO shares for $9 per share on February 15, 1987.

Dan has neither sold nor purchased any TCO stock since he learned of the acquisition plan.

1. What, if any, are the liabilities of ACO under SEC rule 16(b)? Discuss.

2. What, if any, are the liabilities of Dan under SEC rule 10b-5? Discuss.

3. What, if any, are the liabilities of Sam under SEC rule 10b-5? Discuss.

4. What, if any are the liabilities of Len under SEC rule 10b-5? Discuss.

IRAC OUTLINE SHEET

(I)	(R)	(A)	(C)

EXAMPLE OF PROPER IRAC OUTLINE

1. LIABILITIES OF ACO (A)

(I)	(R)	(A)	(C)
16(b)	Jurisdiction	TCO a corporation All sales & purchases described conducted through a nat'l stock exchange	No Violation
	Insider Officer Director 10% s'holder	On 12-1 -86, A bought 120,000 TCO shares for $5 per share thereby becoming a 12% s'holder A never previously owned any TCO stock	
	Short Swing Profit Within 6 Mos	On 12-1 -86, A purchased 120,000 TCO shares for $5 per share 2-15-87, A sold its TCO shares for $9 per share $4 profit per share	
	Purchase/Sale of Equity Security	12-1-86 purchase TCO stock 2-15-87 sale of TCO stock	

2. LIABILITIES OF DAN(D)

(I)	(R)	(A)	(C)
10b-5	Jurisdiction (Instrumentality of Interstate Commerce)	All sales & purchases described conducted through a nat'l stock exchange	Violation
	Omission	A immediately notified TCO's CEO, D, that it made the purchase & that it was considering a tender for the rest of TCO's stock at $9 per share The next day, L, D's personal lawyer, warned D not to buy TCO stock until ACO's stock purchase acquisition plans became public On the same day, D told his son, S about the proposed acquisition On 12-3-86, L&S each bought 10,000 TCO shares for $5 per share (no disclosure)	
	Material	12-3-86, L&S each bought 10,000 TCO shares for $5 per 12-4-86, public disclosure 12-5-86, stock sold for $8.50 per	
	Scienter	D was warned by L his personal lawyer not to buy On the same day, D told his son, S about the proposed acquisition L&S each bought supra	
	Standing	SEC	
	Reliance	See material supra	
	Privity	None	
	Remedies	D is TCO's CEO D did not trade D told S supra (tipper?) S bought 10,000 shares at $5 per S sold 10,000 shares at $8.50 Damages $35,000 as to S only	

3. LIABILITIES OF SAM (S)

(I)	(R)	(A)	(C)
10b-5	Jurisdiction	Supra	Violation
	Omission	D told S about the proposed acquisition plans, supra 12-3-86, S bought 10,000 TCO shares for $5 per share (no disclosure)	

(I)	(R)	(A)	(C)
	Material	Supra	
	Scienter	D told S supra S bought supra	
	Standing	SEC	
	Reliance	Supra	
	Privity	Supra	
	Remedies	D told S supra S is D's son (tippee) D is TCO's CEO S bought/sold supra Damages $35,000	

4. <u>LIABILITIES OF LEN (L)</u>

(I)	(R)	(A)	(C)
<u>10b-5</u>	Jurisdiction	Supra	Arguable
	Omission	D's personal lawyer, L, warned D supra 12-3-86, L bought supra (no disclosure)	
	Material	Supra	
	Scienter	L warned D supra L bought supra	
	Standing	SEC	
	Reliance	Supra	
	Privity	Supra	
	Remedies	L is D's personal lawyer, warned D supra (tippee?) Len bought/sold supra Damages $35,000	

EXAMPLE OF IRAC CORPORATIONS ISSUE

(I) **Liabilities Of ACO Under SEC Rule 16(b)**

(R) Short swing profits realized in connection with the (1) purchase and sale of equity securities listed on a national stock exchange by (2) an officer/director/or holders of more than 10% stock of the corporation within (3) six months of the transaction are recoverable by the corporation.

(A) TCO is a corporation whose (1) stock sales and purchases are conducted on a national stock exchange. This satisfies section 16(b)'s jurisdictional requirement that the corporation be listed on a national exchange.

On December l, 1986, ACO purchased 120,000 TCO shares for $5 per share, thereby becoming a 12%, TCO shareholder. However, ACO had never previously owned any TCO stock prior to this initial transaction. ACO was not (2) an officer, director or 10% shareholder at the time of the purchase in question. Thus, ACO is not the type of insider covered by the SEC Rule 16(b).

By selling these same equity security shares on February 15, 1987 for $9 per share, ACO realized a $4 short swing profit. These profits were realized within (3) the six months of the transaction period covered by 16(b). However, absent ACO's status as an insider, it is not bound to disgorge these profits to TCO corporation.

(C) ACO is not liable for a SEC 16(b) violation.

SUGGESTED MODEL ANSWER

1. LIABILITIES OF ACO UNDER SEC Rule 16(b)

Short swing profits realized in connection with the purchase and sale of equity securities listed on a national stock exchange by an officer/director/or holders of more than 10% stock of the corporation within six months of the transaction are recoverable by the corporation.

TCO is a corporation whose stock sales and purchases are conducted on a national stock exchange. This satisfies Section 16(b)'s jurisdictional requirement that the corporation be listed on a national exchange.

On December 1, 1986, ACO purchased 120,000 TCO shares for $5 per share thereby becoming a 12% TCO shareholder. However, ACO had never previously owned any TCO stock prior to this initial transaction. ACO was not an officer, director or 10% shareholder at the time of the purchase in question. Thus, ACO is not the type of insider covered by the SEC Rule 16(b).

By selling these same equity security shares on February 15, 1987 for $9 per share, ACO realized a $4 short swing profit. These profits were realized within the six months of the transaction period covered by 16(b). However, absent ACO's status as an insider, it is not bound to disgorge these profits to TCO corporation.

ACO is not liable for a SEC 16(b) violation

2. LIABILITIES OF DAN UNDER SEC Rule 10B-5

SEC Rule 10b-5 states that it is unlawful for any person, directly or indirectly, by use of any means or instrumentality of interstate commerce or the mails, to employ any fraudulent or manipulative devices in connection with the purchase or sale of securities.

All sales and purchases of TCO stock were conducted through a national stock exchange. These transactions, if conducted through the mail or on the telephone, will satisfy the jurisdictional requirement pertaining to the use of an instrumentality of interstate commerce.

ACO immediately notified Dan, TCO's executive officer, of its purchase. ACO also notified Dan that it was considering a tender offer for the rest of TCO's stock at $9 per share. Because this information was known only by TCO and Dan, it is considered inside information and Dan must keep the information confidential until it is made public.

The next day, Len, Dan's personal lawyer, warned Dan not to buy TCO stock until ACO's stock purchase acquisition became public. Len's warning indicates that Dan knew that he must not disclose ACO's plans.

On the same day, Dan told his son, Sam, about ACO's proposed acquisition plans. Dan failed to tell him of Len's warning not to buy the stock until the plans had become public.

On December 3, 1986, one day after Dan told Sam and Len about ACO's plans to acquire the rest of TCO's stock for $9 per share, both Sam and Len bought 10,000 TCO shares for $5 per share. They bought the stock without disclosing the inside information to the sellers resulting in an omission to the public.

A reasonable investor would rely on disclosures or lack thereof when making investment decisions. Once the tender offer became public, the price of the stock increased to $8.50. Thus, there is a substantial likelihood that proper disclosure by Sam and Len would have been considered material to a reasonable investor.

Dan disclosed ACO's plans to Len while Len was acting in the capacity of Dan's personal lawyer. Dan was warned by his personal attorney, Len, not to buy any TCO stock. Dan did not do so. Due to the attorney/client fiduciary relationship, Len's trading was unforeseeable. Dan would not be deemed to have had scienter as to Len's dealings.

However, he told Sam about ACO's plans and Sam bought the stock. Dan's disclosure was highly reckless since it would foreseeably result in Sam's actions. Therefore, Dan acted with scienter.

The SEC is a governmental body charged with the power to pursue litigation against defendants who have violated the Federal Exchange Securities Act. The SEC has standing to sue Dan.

Reliance is usually presumed when materiality has been shown. However, where an omission has occurred, as in this case, the court has dispensed with the element of reliance.

The SEC no longer requires that one must prove privity in order to sue.

Dan was TCO's chief executive officer. His position created a fiduciary duty to TCO to refrain from disclosing inside information. Since Dan possessed nonpublic information, he will be considered an insider who will be held responsible for any disclosures he makes.

Dan did not deal on the information. However, his son, Sam did. Dan should have known that when he disclosed the information to his son, Sam would exploit that information for his personal gain. Therefore, Dan will be liable as a tipper for damages in the amount of the difference between the $5 per share purchase price and the $8.50 per share sales price multiplied by the 10,000 shares sold.

Dan will be liable for $35,000. However, as to Len, no liability will attach.

3. LIABILITIES OF SAM UNDER SEC Rule 10B-5

Defined supra.

Jurisdiction has been previously proven. Sam learned about ACO's proposed acquisition plans when Dan told him about them. Pursuant to that, Sam bought 10,000 shares for $5 a share on December 3, 1986. His failure to disclose this nonpublic information to the seller from whom Sam made the purchase was an omission.

The seller sold shares to Sam at $5 per share unaware that their value would increase due to the tender offer plans of ACO. This conduct shows that the failure to disclose would effect whether a reasonable investor would have sold for that price. Since Sam then sold the same shares for $8.50 per share on December 5, 1986, the omission was clearly material.

After Dan told him about TCO's plans, Sam knew that ACO's acquisition plans would undoubtedly increase the value of the stock. His haste in buying the stock after being told of the plans shows his intent to take advantage of this inside information. Therefore, his failure to disclose information before buying was done with scienter.

Standing and reliance can be established as previously discussed.

Sam learned of TCO's plans from his father, Dan. Thus, Sam is a non-insider. Since Dan was TCO's CEO, Dan breached his fiduciary duty to his corporate employer. Further, Sam should have known that any nonpublic information he learned from his father would constitute a breach of Dan's fiduciary duty to TCO. Sam would be considered a tippee.

Sam will be liable, as a tippee, for the difference between his purchase and sales price.

Sam will be liable for $35,000.

4. LIABILITIES OF LEN UNDER SEC Rule 10B-5

Defined supra.

Jurisdiction has been previously proven. Like Sam, Len also failed to disclose the information he learned about TCO's acquisition plans from Dan. Instead, he acted on the information by buying 10,000 shares. As previously discussed under the liabilities of Sam, Len's failure to disclose was an omission. Materiality can also be shown as previously discussed.

Since Len warned Dan not to buy TCO stock until the acquisition plans were made public, he clearly knew that to do so would be improper. Thus, when Len himself acted on the inside information, his intent clearly demonstrated scienter.

Standing and reliance have been previously proven.

Len was Dan's personal lawyer. Since he had no direct individual or fiduciary duty to TCO, he was not an insider. However, as Dan's personal lawyer, Len would know that by acting on Dan's information, he would cause a breach of Dan's fiduciary duty to TCO. Len would be deemed a tippee.

Len would counter that Dan would never foresee that Len would act on information disclosed during the attorney-client relationship. Dan did not breach his fiduciary duty to TCO by seeking legal advice from Len. If so, Dan is not a tipper. Therefore, Len is not a tippee.

In addition, Len would contend that he acquired the information as part of his business dealings. As such, it was a mere acquisition of knowledge insufficient to impose liability.

However, this knowledge was gained as a result of an attorney-client relationship. It goes well beyond a mere acquisition of information. Len obtained this nonpublic information improperly by misappropriating the information resulting in a breach of the attorney/client privilege. Thus, Len should be liable for the difference between the purchase and sale price of the shares.

Len will be liable for $35,000.